A Wonderful Life

Also by Cyrus M. Copeland

Farewell, Godspeed: The Greatest Eulogies of Our Time

A WONDERFUL LIFE

50 Eulogies to Lift the Spirit

EDITED BY

CYRUS M. COPELAND

Algonquin Books of Chapel Hill

2006

Published by
Algonquin Books of Chapel Hill
Post Office Box 2225
Chapel Hill, North Carolina 27515-2225

a division of
Workman Publishing
708 Broadway
New York, New York 10003

For permission to reprint material included in this book, grateful
acknowledgment is made to the copyright holders mentioned on
pages 293–296, which constitute an extension of the copyright page.

Library of Congress Cataloging-in-Publication Data
   A wonderful life : 50 eulogies to lift the spirit / edited by
Cyrus M. Copeland.—1st ed.
        p. cm.
     ISBN-13: 978-1-56512-511-7; ISBN-10: 1-56512-511-8
     1. Eulogies.   2. Celebrities—Biography.   I. Copeland,
Cyrus.
CT105.W66 2006
820.02—dc22
   [B]   2005057030

10 9 8 7 6 5 4 3 2 1
FIRST EDITION

FOR KATAYOUN

Longtime witness to my life, teller of stories, lifter of spirits

Do not stand on my grave and weep
I am not there I do not sleep
I am a thousand winds that blow
I am the diamond glints in the snow
I am the sunlight on ripened grain
I am a gentle autumn's rain
When you awaken in the morning hush
I am the swift uplifting rush
I am the birds in circled flight
I am the soft stars that shine at night
So do not stand on my grave and cry
I am not there
I did not die

—MELINDA SUE PACHO

CONTENTS

Contents

Contents

FOREWORD

Throughout the mid-twentieth century, former vaudevillian George Jessel was the acknowledged king of the eulogy. To have Jessel deliver one of his florid funereal send-offs was proof that, at the time of his or her earthly departure, the deceased had really arrived.

Sprinkling kudos, exhausting, depleting, mining, and milking every known thesaurus, Jessel would heap encomiums upon his subjects by the shovelful, however crude the analogy.

So frequent were his stand-ups alongside those who were lying down, it was rumored Jessel could be compensated for his compassion; that his praise could be bought by the pound. And why not? Whereas his income had been greatly diminished when vaudeville died, mortality never has shown the slightest sign of going out of business.

Bolstering the suspicion that his empathy might indeed have had a price tag attached was the instance in which Jessel, extolling the virtues of the encased gentleman with whom he was sharing the stage, praised the man's excellence as a husband, as a father, a patriot, a philanthropist nonpareil, making his subject sound as though he was eligible for instant elevation to sainthood.

Enraptured by his own eloquence, almost airsick from the loftiness of his prose, Jessel paused a moment, lowered his eyes, and gazed at the open coffin. Shocked by a sudden realization, he looked out at the assembled and announced: "My God, I know this man."

Having arrived at an age where every open grave is a "gimme," I find myself increasingly called upon to speak at memorial services for far too many people that I have not only known but that I deeply respected and admired; some that I can truly say I loved.

In creating a picture of the unwitting guest of honor, I find it best to avoid both the portentous and the politic. A few simple truths are all that's required. It's not necessary to work in oils; the lighter the stroke, the better. An honest, last public appraisal of a friend's life needn't sound as though it should be accompanied by strings. Don't embarrass the departed with praise that is too fulsome. Don't make it seem to the assembled that, at the very last moment, they are saying farewell to someone they never really knew.

Also to be avoided is the sense of upstaging the most captive member of your audience, the star of the occasion, after all. A eulogy is not meant to be a vehicle for self-aggrandizement. Try pressing the shift key as little as possible when typing the letter *i*. In addition to checking one's spelling and grammar, employing an ego check is a pretty good idea, too.

Most important: respect needs no repetition; sincerity shrinks when stretched. As brevity is the soul of wit, it can—make that should—also be the soul of gravity.

—*Larry Gelbart*
CUERNAVACA, MEXICO

INTRODUCTION

A decade ago, I delivered my father's eulogy. Talk to anyone who has delivered a eulogy and you will be told what I'm going to tell you now: It was a cathartic, connective experience. Through the tears, I was gratified to have done it.

Afterward, I had the idea to organize a book of eulogies for our cultural heroes—a kind of front-row seat at their memorials. To my surprise, there were no such books. So I did what we all do with those occasional flashes of creative inspiration: Nothing.

The years passed, and I continued my job in advertising, selling everything from Halls cough drops to HBO.

But I am a New Yorker. And in the days after 9/11, life changed. I could not leave my apartment without passing a church and hearing one, two, five eulogies a day to fallen firemen, policemen, those newfound American heroes, and suddenly the idea to do a collection of eulogies to our heroes was rekindled. I left my job and cushy expense account. I got an agent and publishing deal in surprisingly short order. And I dedicated myself to studying the art of remembrance.

When *Farewell, Godspeed* was published, I savored the rush of recognition: Not just in the press (the *New York Times*! the *Boston Globe*!) or printings (six, thank you) but also, more personally, in the e-mails people sent, which always said one of two things: I had no idea eulogies were so uplifting, or, this book made me think about how I'd be remembered.

Today, I'm happy to raise the dead once again. *A Wonderful Life* pays tribute to our heroes—but it is also simply, unabashedly, about the joy of a well-lived life.

Elisabeth Kübler-Ross lived with legendary abandon. She said if you live each day of your life right, you have nothing to fear from death. Inspired, I wrote to Ms. Ross's son, wondering if I could include her eulogy in my first book. He replied, "Thank you for your note. I am somewhat confused however—my mother has not made her 'transition' yet and we are going shopping today. Are you bidding her farewell before she 'checks out'? Please clarify."

Ouch!

After recounting the episode to my friends, who shared a laugh—a common occurrence, since my traffic in graveside chats produces even more unintended humor than a career in advertising—I sent an apology to her son, who advised me not to worry; people are always thinking she died, or converted to Buddhism, or something—and that I could eventually include her in the sequel to *Farewell, Godspeed*.

Which I have. Safely dead, Ms. Kübler-Ross still inspires. "It is not for us to say that she has died," her eulogizer observed, "but to say, 'God did she live!' For being the legendary expert on death and dying, she was the most alive person I ever met."

Here are fifty tributes to extraordinary lives. Elisabeth Kübler-Ross to Charlie Chaplin. Lenny Bruce to Gandhi.

Lenny Bruce and Gandhi? That is the point of great eulogies. At the eleventh hour, our differences fade away and we concentrate on what really matters about a life. We don't talk about what they looked like. How many awards they won. Their professional accomplishments. Their politics. Not the stats—which is really the business of obituaries—but rather the *essence* of a life.

When I set out to compose my father's eulogy, I could hear his voice in my head telling me this was a joyful moment. And I knew that somehow he was *there* in a different, nonimaginary way. I knew it. It was a kind of bridge that stretched across the chasm of his absence in my life.

And that is what a good eulogy can be: A bridge between the living and the dead, between *us* and *them,* memory and eternity, my memories of my dad and a lifetime that stretches forward without him. A great eulogy assures us that our loved ones will endure in our collective memories. The more specific and real the remembrances spoken, the stronger the bridge.

"There may be little or much beyond the grave," Robert Frost wrote, "but the strong are saying nothing 'til they see." Frost was wrong. Miked and suited and taking the floor, the strong are saying plenty.

—*Cyrus M. Copeland*

A Wonderful Life

MOVIE STARS

BETTE DAVIS

By David Hartman, friend and longtime admirer

DELIVERED AT MEMORIAL SERVICE, NOVEMBER 2, 1989
WARNER BROS. SOUNDSTAGE 18, HOLLYWOOD

A wise man told me the most a person can say about his or her life is, "I was here! I mattered!" Well, goodness knows, Bette Davis was here. And she mattered.

Ralph Waldo Emerson, who spent most of his life just a few miles from where Bette was raised, understood the New England spirit of which Bette was so proud. Emerson wrote, "Nothing is at last sacred but the integrity of your own mind. To believe your own thought, to believe that what is true for you in your private heart is true for all men—that is genius . . . imitation is suicide . . . Accept the place divine providence has found for you."

He could have been writing about Bette. She not only accepted her place—the one she made—she relished it. She trumpeted it. Celebrated it. And I hope she would want us, along with our tears, to also celebrate her place, her legacy, tonight.

Bette's legacy is certainly her work. So what an appropriate place to have this memorial tribute: On a no-frills, undecorated (except with Bette) working soundstage where she made six movies: *Kid Galahad, The Letter, Now Voyager, Old Acquaintance, A Stolen Life,* and *Winter Meeting.*

Bette said, "The person who wants to make it has to sweat! There are no shortcuts. And you've got to have the guts to be hated—that's the hard part. It's only the work that truly satisfies. I think I've known this all my life. No one could ever share my drive or visions. No one has ever understood the sweetness of my job at the end of a good day's work."

Maybe not, Bette. But tonight each of us has the opportunity to remember the Bette we knew, celebrate how you matter to us, and recall the work that gave you such sweet joy—and such dignity—and so many awards.

Many say that the Kennedy Center Honors have become the most prestigious of American awards because they span the breadth of culture in recognizing lifetime achievement in the performing arts. On December 5, 1987, Bette became a Kennedy Center honoree. I had the pleasure of presenting her that evening, and I'd like to share that presentation with you now, and the toast I made to her.

"The night before I met Bette the first time, I was apprehensive. No, that's a lie! I was nervous. What would the real Bette Davis be like? I'd heard all the words to describe her: Tough, strong, proud, opinionated, perfectionist, ferocious, larger-than-life, intimidating. I thought tomorrow morning might be a tough one.

"In she strode. One of my coworkers, as a thoughtful gesture, started to take a white thread from Bette's dark skirt. In vintage

Davis, Bette intones, 'Don't touch that thread! Bad luck.' There she was! The real Bette Davis. Five feet two inches of dynamite.

"One critic wrote, 'Bette Davis would probably have been burned as a witch if she had lived two or three hundred years ago. She gives the curious feeling of being charged with power that can find no ordinary outlet.' Good thing she found the movie screen. She once told me that some people are sugar, some are vinegar. She's vinegar. Maybe. But so much more: New England Yankee. Disciplined, honest, hard worker, never puts on airs, tells it like it is, always gives 100 percent. Like the needlepoint pillow at her home says: 'No guts, no glory.' Especially these last few years she has shown, it seems, extra strength, courage, and dignity, and she can always laugh at herself. She tells about leaving the studio on the first day of suspension. Jack Warner said, 'Bette, don't leave. We just bought a new book for you. It's called *Gone with the Wind*.' Bette's parting shot: 'Yah, Jack, and I'll just bet it's a pip.'

"Bette, as the globe has changed so much over the past five decades, you have been constant for hundreds of millions of us who have ever walked into a movie theater or now can cram a cassette into a VCR. Thank you for showing up at work, for doing it so well, for sharing your power with us. We hope your career has been as fulfilling and gratifying for you as it has been wonderful for us.

"We applaud you, we salute you, we love you.

"God bless you."

1908 Born Ruth Elizabeth Davis, in the middle of an electrical storm, in Lowell, Mass.

1915 Her parents divorce. Defying convention, her mother raises two daughters alone at the turn of the century.

1928 Debuts on Broadway in *Broken Dishes*, age 21. Impressed, a Universal executive signs Bette and invites her to Hollywood—but thinking her too homely to be an actress, the studio gofer leaves Bette at the train station.

1932 Breakthrough film: *The Man Who Played God.* Warner Bros. signs Davis to a long-term contract, beginning her stormy 18-year relationship with the studio more accustomed to promoting its male stars. In an era of classically beautiful stars, Davis survives by sheer force of her personality, talent, and well-known mannerisms—including clipped New England diction and extravagant cigarette smoking.

1935 Wins her first Oscar for *Dangerous,* followed three years later by another Oscar for *Jezebel.* Reputedly gives Oscar its nickname, joking it reminded her of "the derriere of my husband [Harmon Oscar Nelson]."

1939 Divorces first husband. Three more follow.

1941 First woman to become president of the Academy of Motion Picture Arts and Sciences.

1942 By now Davis is the highest-paid woman in America—frequently referred to as "the Fifth Warner." Opens the Hollywood Canteen for U.S. military men, transforming an abandoned nightclub into a top-tier hospitality center. Davis: "There are few accomplishments in my life that I am sincerely proud of. The Hollywood Canteen is one of them."

1950 Bounces back from forgettable string of films with *All About Eve*—based on tempestuous star Tallulah Bankhead. Delivers unforgettable line, "Fasten your seatbelts, it's going to be a bumpy ride!"

1962 Her career takes an unexpected twist again with *Whatever Happened to Baby Jane?* On the set, she and Crawford continue their well-documented rivalry, but the movie earns Davis her tenth Oscar nomination. Takes out a tongue-in-cheek ad in *Hollywood Reporter*: "Situation Wanted: Mother of three, 30 years experience as an actress, more affable than rumor would have it, wants steady employment in Hollywood."

1976 Launches decade-long television career with *The Disappearance of Aimee*. Subsequently wins Emmy for *Strangers* (1979), *Little Gloria . . . Happy at Last* (1982), and *A Piano for Mrs. Cimino* (1982).

1978 First woman to receive the American Film Institute Lifetime Achievement Award.

1989 Dies in Paris, after a protracted and defiant battle with cancer. With a career spanning six decades and 100 films, 80 awards, four marriages, three children, Davis appropriately chose the following epitaph: "She Did It the Hard Way."

JUDY GARLAND

By James Mason, friend and colleague

DELIVERED AT FUNERAL, JUNE 27, 1969
THE CAMPBELL FUNERAL HOME, NEW YORK CITY

The thing about Judy Garland was that she was so alive. You close your eyes and you see a small, vivid woman, sometimes fat, sometimes thin, but vivid. Vivacity, vitality— that's what our Judy had and still has as far as I'm concerned. I did not see much of her during the last ten years. Maybe she was low or sick or not at the top of her form, but it did not in the least impair the unbreakable image which remained constant, up to and including today.

Beyond the walls of this church there are millions of people in the United States who know Judy Garland and love her, and there are millions more in other countries; each individual cherishes his hantly returns to film in *A Star Is Born*.

....

l by weight gain and throat troubles, Garland suffers from hepati-
e result of sleeping pills, pep pills, diet pills, and nerve tonics pre-
by the studio to either invigorate or tranquilize her. Hollywood
her unemployable.

....

back again with spectacular, sobbing, back-to-back performances
egie Hall.

....

heels of a failed TV series, Garland contemplates retiring to de-
rself to her three children. Marries her fourth husband, Mark
divorcing him shortly thereafter. "I feel like I'm living in a bliz-
ne says.

....

e stage in London, but is unable to finish her run.

....

London, 47, from a drug overdose—found on the bathroom
her husband of three months, Mickey Deans. Survived by her
ildren, Garland left a legacy of compulsively hopeful heroines
ng that mirrored the elusive happiness she never attained in her

....

own special image. Each such image is registered firmly in a living brain; each one alive. And those images will remain alive until in turn each life is switched off and its memory fades. When the youngest of those who today love Judy is no longer alive, only then will the idea of Judy as we know her be finally rendered extinct, and she will become instead a chapter in the history of show business.

Those who read this chapter will wonder what she was and will ask why contemporaries raved about her and carried on so.

There is a German saying worth quoting: "Posterity weaves no garlands for actors."

It may seem ironic that some of our newspapers and magazines are prepared to devote more space to this final event than to any of Judy's achievements during her life. But let's not fret too much about that. Let us make the best of the moment and weave garlands while we may. If only for the sake of the future student of show-business history who will try to make something of that chapter that survives of Judy, let us define this lady's greatness.

Tonight in Hollywood, veterans will reminisce deep into the night about the teenage Judy in her early days at MGM. There are many here in this church, I am sure, who witnessed her rebirth as a star at the Palace Theater in 1951. I was thrilled by the echoes that reverberated in California, but I remained a witness by hearsay only.

I traveled in her orbit only for a while, but it was an exciting while, and one during which the joys in her life out-balanced the miseries. The little girl whom I knew who had a little curl right in the middle of her forehead, when she was good she was not only very, very good, she was the most sympathetic, the funniest, the sharpest, and the most stimulating woman I ever knew.

She was a lady who gave so much and richly, both to her vast audience whom she entertained and to the friends around her whom she loved so that there was no currency in which to repay her. And she needed to be repaid, she needed devotion and love beyond the resources of any of us.

People took from her what they wanted most. Had I ever been in a position to take what I wanted from her, it would have been a long program of funny movies, since I firmly believed that she was the funniest girl in the world. But she was so touching that she was invariably in demand to do the purely emotional thing. It was this very touching quality that made her such a great comedian. In these great funny films that I dreamed of she would have developed a line of whacky comedy which would have been more effective being played without a trace of emotion in the framework of a harrowing plot.

She had pursued this line very effectively, if briefly, during the early stages of her movie career. But the lines had been discontinued, and the hopes for its revival which I long cherished must now at last be abandoned.

I think that I have a hint for the Judy Garland student yet unborn. Her special talent was this: She could sing so that it would break your heart. What is a tough audience? A tough audience is a group of high-income-bracket cynics at a Hollywood party. Judy's gift to them was to wring tears from men with hearts of rock.

—∞∞—

1922 Born Frances Gumm, to vaudeville parents.

1930 Addicted to the sound of applause, Frances is pulled from a Christmas lineup by her own father, after singing *Jingle Bells* seven times straight. Continues performing with her sisters Suzanne and Virginia, until their act is accidentally billed as the "Glum Sisters."

1934 Her father dies when she is 12.

1936 Taking her mother's maiden na[...]
promptly debuting in *Pigskin Pa[...]*
make her a star.

1939 *The Wizard of Oz* catapults her [...]
sings "Over the Rainbow"—a [...]
echo her own fruitless search.

1940 The pressures of stardom sen[...]
$150,000/picture at age 20, G[...]
bed, dashing over to the doct[...]
couch, telling my troubles to a [...]
swered in an accent I couldn't [...]
make movie love to Mickey R[...]

1943 Begins taking stimulants and [...]
they'd take us to the studio h[...]
pills. After four hours they'd v[...]
the way we worked, and that [...]
got mixed up. And that's the [...]

1945 Marries gay director Vincente [...]
ishes. *Meet Me in St. Louis* co[...]
Clock, which earns her praise[...]

1949 Fails to report to work on th[...]

1950 Attempts suicide for the firs[...]
She returns to the stage, div[...]
with laryngitis, retains the fu[...]
York Times: "That the voice i[...]
Judy is great."

1954 Triump[...]

1959 Plague[...]
tis—th[...]
scribe[...]
deems[...]

1960 Comes[...]
at Car[...]

1965 On the [...]
vote h[...]
Herror[...]
zard," s[...]

1968 Takes t[...]

1969 Dies in [...]
floor by[...]
three c[...]
and a s[...]
own life[...]

MARILYN MONROE

By Donald Spoto, biographer

DELIVERED AT MEMORIAL EVENING, AUGUST 5, 1992
WESTWOOD MEMORIAL CEMETERY, LOS ANGELES

The untimely death of a beautiful woman is one of the oldest romantic conventions in art and literature, running from the Greek tragic heroine Alcestis through Hamlet's Ophelia to some of the real-life models chosen by the pre-Raphaelite painters, to Poe's Annabel Lee. These women, whether real or fictional, died for art or for love.

Marilyn Monroe died for neither.

Our Marilyn wasn't the beginning of the great untimely deaths, but she might have been the last. She was certainly the last of a wonderful kind. She came to prominence at a green and crazy time in American life and culture. Held in subtle contempt by her Hollywood employers and burdened with mostly inept and inappropriate roles, she was in a way doomed to be seen by the studios and much of the public as a joke—the quintessence of the dumb blonde.

The joke is on us. She was a woman of extraordinary talent—not just beautiful, but also witty, a child of nature with a native intelligence—not just sexy but savvy about the ways of men and moguls. Still, she was victimized by the tabloid mentality that began to flourish after World War II and that has wounded so many people (some, to be sure, were willing victims). Never mind that Marilyn overcame a wretched childhood and was determined to make something worthwhile of herself; never mind, too, that she wanted to work hard and be taken seriously. Now as then, we don't want to hear about all that, otherwise perhaps we have to revise our thinking and—horrors!—respect her.

From the late 1940s to her death in 1962, Marilyn lit up our culture, but we were all somewhat schizoid about her. In a way, we wanted her to fail, wanted her to come deliberately to a bad end, and if she would not indeed do this on her own—as she certainly did not—well, then, some people just made up the stories of her filthy habits and of her eventual destruction at the hands of this or that powerful public figure. What nonsense. But it was easy to foist on the public, who presumed she couldn't be any good—after all, she was a beautiful, sexy, successful, and much loved woman, and the American-puritan ethos had to regard her as Eve, if not Mata Hari.

More to the point, something in us wants celebrities, especially the rich and the handsome, to collapse under the weight of their fame. By a kind of totemic selfishness, something in us does not object when the miseries of life are visited on the rich and the famous; something in us wants those who are wealthy and beautiful to demonstrate for us that wealth, fame, and beauty are transient and unimportant. And it's much better if they do this in a violent way and involve others in their perfidy. Marilyn didn't go along with this rubbish, but she has been saddled with it for a longer time than she lived.

Hollywood, ever alert to our longings, knows that we have an innate need to adore. America has no royal family, and so the studios gave us Clark Gable, "The King," and John Wayne, "The Duke." There have been several men called "Prince." And Marilyn — the ultimate movie queen. An icon. An icon in the sense that she points us elsewhere, showing us not just our possibilities, but also our yearnings and our failures, our frailties and our unmet needs. She shows us where to look for them, and where to avoid. Marilyn Monroe was just like us, only more so.

We ask too much of Marilyn Monroe; if we do not hold her in contempt, we want to adore her. She was no goddess, and she laughed when words like that were used. She ought to be simply and purely the object of love — not adoration — for all the fun she gave us in her movies.

She was once asked her goal in life. "I just want to be wonderful," she replied quietly.

And so you were, Marilyn — and so you were.

1926 Born Norma Jean Mortenson in Los Angeles — to a poor, single mother who brings home a plethora of men, confusing Norma Jean about her actual father.

1935 Left by her mother in a series of foster homes. The L.A. Orphan's Home pays Norma Jean a nickel a month, then takes a penny back every Sunday for church. Later, she describes her childhood as "Oliver Twist in girls' clothing."

1941 Leaving high school, she works in an aircraft plant at sixteen. Marries a man she calls Daddy.

1946 Divorces Daddy. Begins modeling. Upon seeing her pictures, RKO head Howard Hughes offers her a screen test—but she goes with prestigious 20th Century Fox, signing for $125/week. Changes her hair to blonde, her name to Marilyn Monroe.

1947 After a series of forgettable bit parts, Fox doesn't renew her contract.

1949 Famously poses nude—a shot that becomes *Playboy*'s first centerfold. The following year, she lands five movies, including *All About Eve*. On screen for just a few minutes, she makes a sizable impression as a ditzy but very sexy blonde, and holds her own against Bette Davis. Her volcanic sexuality wrapped in childlike wonder erupts. Fox re-signs her to a seven-year contract.

1952 Filming *Gentlemen Prefer Blondes,* Monroe is told she is not the star. Replies, "Well whatever I am, I'm still the blonde." The image she cultivates is at odds with her extraordinarily high IQ; Monroe secretly reads Whitman, Tolstoy, and Milton, and frequently carries around *The Biography of Abraham Lincoln* for inspiration.

1954 Marries baseball legend Joe DiMaggio. Divorces DiMaggio. Although their union lasted only eight months, "he treated me like something special."

1955 Winning streak continues with *The Seven Year Itch,* featuring one of the most memorable scenes in movie history: Marilyn standing atop a subway grate, skirt blowing scandalously. She receives 5,000 letters/week. But her work habits slide: Continually late on set and frequently ill, Monroe becomes a liability, at odds with actors and directors.

1956 Stuns the critics with dramatic turn in *Bus Stop,* and the press with her marriage to playwright Arthur Miller.

1958 After a year off, returns to the screen in frothy *Some Like It Hot*—a smash with Tony Curtis and Jack Lemmon.

1961 Makes *The Misfits,* her final movie. Monroe is exhausted, and filming is frequently halted. Divorces Miller.

1962 Famously serenades JFK on his birthday. Begins filming the portentous *Something's Gotta Give,* but frequently shows up late (if at all) and is fired. In seclusion in her L.A. home, Monroe overdoses on sedatives and is found by her housekeeper—dead at 36, her life ending as it began, in tragedy. The quintessential golden girl whose success never translated to happiness, Monroe left the bulk of her estate to acting coach Lee Strasberg—and a legacy of 30 movies to a still-adoring public, who continue to document, discuss, and dissect her life.

CHARLIE CHAPLIN

By Jerry Epstein, collaborator and close friend

WRITTEN IN COMMEMORATION

Charlie was always curious, never blasé. That was the secret of his eternal youth. In London, when we went to pantomimes and music halls together, we'd behave like kids. He'd love to peer through restaurant windows and count the number of customers. "If it's full, it must be good!" he'd say.

Sometimes he took me and Oona to dingy hovels. He never forgot his roots. Disappearing among the crowds, he'd hop on a bus and watch the passing parade through the window. Of course, he enjoyed the other side of life—limousines, luxury—but he remained unaffected by his fame. He never thought he should be treated any differently than anyone else.

In Los Angeles he showed *The Great Dictator* for a charity performance. When I arrived at the theater on Wilshire Boulevard, the lines stretched around the block, and as I walked around the corner I saw Oona and Charlie lined up with all the others. "What are you doing, standing in line for your own picture?" I said and rushed them towards the box office. He always refused to take advantage of his position.

Although Charlie was wealthy, he was never ostentatious. His childhood years had made an indelible impression on him; besides, he'd worked too hard to squander his money. (Sydney, his eldest son, on the other hand, was different. To him, money was meant to be spent. Charlie was appalled. "Easy come, easy go," he'd say. And Syd would answer, "I can't help it, I was born with a silver spoon in my mouth. If you'd been born like me, maybe you'd be a big spender too!") Without advertising the fact, Charlie looked after many old-timers and actresses and kept them on his payroll throughout their lives.

On special occasions Oona and Charlie enjoyed nothing better than celebrating along with a bottle of champagne and a tin of the finest caviar. But he'd always say, "If you did this every day, the fun would soon be gone." He did things in moderation.

Charlie was always able to tell when certain actors were suc-cumbing to their newfound wealth. He'd say, "They're beginning to act like insurance salesmen!" The vitality, spark, and energy that first brought them into the limelight was gone—and it had noth-ing to do with age. Charlie never became like this. When certain actresses won Academy Awards and everyone raved about their tal-ents, he'd look at them coldly and say, "Even if they were good, I wouldn't like them." Something about their personalities rubbed him the wrong way.

He was always aware of the public. While at the Manoir in 1954, a friend visited him and brought a record of a new singer called Elvis Presley. Charlie hadn't heard of him. "This man has made a sensation in the States!" the friend said. "I can't understand it. He wiggles his hips and sings and people go mad." "If he's made such an impact," Charlie replied, "he must have something. You can't fool the public."

I never saw Charlie depressed. I saw him anxious, tense, but never down. I was always amazed how, in the face of adversity, he was able to pick himself up and get on with living. For him, each new day was a day full of challenge and promise. "Don't wish your life away," he'd say when Oona or I were eagerly awaiting some big event, "enjoy the moment."

Charlie may not have been very tall, but when he came into a room, he seemed to tower over everyone else. Even if you didn't know who he was, you'd be aware you were looking at a man of importance. People often asked me what he was like in real life. "See his films and you'll know," I'd reply. Everything he did on the screen was a facet of himself. I think that's why people all over the world identified with him.

After meeting Ingmar Bergman in Sweden, Charlie gave an interview to the *Herald Tribune,* and said he never missed an Ingmar Bergman film. The paper printed it as "an Ingrid Bergman film." She was thrilled, and in subsequent interviews she quoted Charlie as saying he never missed one of her films. Charlie was too much of a gentleman to refute the lady.

Charlie often said he would never have achieved such worldwide success if he had stayed in England. There, he was up against a social barrier that impedes advancement. Americans never ask, "Where do you come from? Are you public schooled?" They are only interested in what you can do and how well you can do it. But in the 1940s and '50s, Charlie was outraged that the American film industry wasn't prepared to unite and take a stand against political witch-hunters. Instead, out of fear, the studio heads capitulated. "They have the most powerful instrument in their hands—the motion picture," Charlie said. "They should have used it to expose these bastards. Instead, they sold out and became weak and mealy-mouthed." But in spite of how he was eventually treated during the witch hunts, Charlie never lost his affection for America. "After all, that's where I met Oona."

His influence on the motion-picture industry has been innovative and far-reaching. Before Charlie, comedy had no real structure. It was a series of chases and gags. He brought it body, form, and most of all, character. He was the first to construct a comic sequence, add complications and milk the situation, until it reached its logical conclusion. Today, the young know the figure of the Tramp, but they are not acquainted with his films. And they should be! Schools should screen Charlie's works as part of cultural studies, alongside musical appreciation and the history of art. His films elevate the spirit and enrich the soul. Television does not do them justice—they should be shown on at least a 16mm movie screen, where the viewer can behold his incredible eyes, the nuances of his gestures, and the stillness of his figure.

I'm proud to have worked with him, and to have known him as a friend.

I miss him.

1889 Born Charles Spencer Chaplin, son of a boozy vaudevillian and a music-hall chanteuse, in London. His father leaves shortly after he is born.

1895 When his mother loses her voice on stage, Chaplin replaces her—captivating the audience, upstaging his mother, and experiencing the first alluring call of applause.

1903 Gets small stage part in a *Sherlock Holmes* play and tours the countryside.

1914 After a decade with a comedy troupe, L.A. producer Mack Sennett signs Chaplin for $150/week. Told by Sennett to wear something comic, Chaplin grabs Fatty Arbuckle's pants, size 14 shoes, a too-tight coat, derby and mustache, adding his endearing shuffle at the last minute. The Little Tramp is born. Chaplin goes on to make 35 films with Sennett.

1915 The Mutual Company signs Chaplin for $670,000/year—a stupendous sum. Continues living in a shabby hotel room and keeping studio checks in his trunk. Just three years out of vaudeville, the 26-year-old remarks, "Well, I've got this much, if they never give me another cent—guess I'll go buy a dozen ties."

1918 Marries 16-year-old Mildred Harris. Divorces her two years later.

1919 Founds United Artists with Hollywood heavies Mary Pickford, Douglas Fairbanks Sr., and D.W. Griffith. When his Mutual contract runs out, Chaplin distributes exclusively through UA—never again to return to the shackles of a studio contract.

1924 Marries 16-year-old Lita Grey. They have two children before divorcing, a process so acrimonious and stressful that Chaplin's hair turns permanently white.

1925 Releases *The Gold Rush*, "the picture I want to be remembered by." In its most famous scene, Chaplin boils, carves, and chews on his shoe with the zest of a gourmand—wringing comedy from poverty and tickling millions.

1931 Releases *City Lights*, his first nonsilent film.

1937 Marries *Modern Times* costar Paulette Goddard. They divorce five years later.

1940 The Little Tramp gives way to Hitler with *The Great Dictator*, an indictment of the Nazi regime. Not content to write, direct, and star, Chaplin also serves as hairdresser. His perfectionism accounts for cost overruns, miles of unused film, and five Oscar nominations.

1943 Marries Oona O'Neill, daughter of playwright Eugene O'Neill—the fourth and arguably happiest of his marriages.

1952 On the heels of income-tax trouble and tabloid feeding frenzies, sporting a reputation as a political radical in Cold War times, Chaplin is virtually deported. He settles in Switzerland on a sprawling 38-acre estate and spends the balance of his life in Europe. "I have no further use for America. I wouldn't go back even if Jesus were president."

1972 Twenty years later, age 83, Chaplin returns to the U.S. for a final engagement—collecting a special Oscar from the Academy. Aged and quiet, the once-ebullient Chaplin blows kisses to the audience, tears running down his face.

1977 Dies in his sleep, on Christmas—the ragamuffin who became preeminent artist of his time, having lifted motion pictures from flickering novelty to high art. His legacy: a Little Tramp who is just looking for romance and a little respect. "That is why, no matter how desperate the predicament is, I always straighten my derby and fix my tie, even though I've just landed on my head." Chaplin is survived by 11 children.

JOAN CRAWFORD

By George Cukor, friend and director

DELIVERED AT MEMORIAL SERVICE, JUNE 24, 1977
SAMUEL GOLDWYN THEATER, LOS ANGELES

I know it sounds off, but somehow I did not believe Joan Crawford could ever die. She was the perfect image of a movie star, and as such largely the creation of her own indomitable will. She had, of course, very remarkable material to work with: a quick native intelligence, tremendous animal vitality, a lovely figure, and above all her face, that extraordinary sculptural construction of lines and planes, finely chiseled like the mask of some classical divinity from fifth-century Greece. It caught the light superbly. You could photograph her from any angle, and the face moved beautifully.

But she was serious with it: serious about improving herself as an actress, serious about her total dedication to screen stardom.

Though she led a busy life off-screen, with husbands, children, and business interests, the career was always central. And she played every role with the same fierce determination, holding back for nothing. In the part of the bitchy, opportunistic girl in *The Women,* she knew perfectly well that she would be surrounded by very formidable competition from the rest of the all-female cast, playing funnier parts and certainly more sympathetic parts, yet she made no appeals for audience sympathy: she was not one of those actresses who have to keep popping out from behind their characters signaling, "Look, it's sweet, lovable me, just pretending to be a tramp." In *A Woman's Face* she played at the outset a disfigured monster of a woman who would not flinch from killing a child, and she did not soften it a bit. Yet in *Susan and God* she found all the comedy in the silly, empty-headed woman who finally, funnily grows to emotional maturity. Whatever she did, she did wholeheartedly.

Including her love affair with the camera. In the days before zoom lenses and advanced electronics, cameras often had to be mounted on great cumbersome cranes, maneuvered by as many as twelve men, and close-ups might well require all this to be pushed from an extreme long shot to within a few inches of an actor's face. Most found it difficult to overcome some understandable nervousness as this juggernaut ground closer and closer. Not Joan Crawford. The nearer the camera, the more tender and yielding she became—her eyes glistened, her lips parted in ecstatic acceptance. The camera saw, I suspect, a side of her that no flesh-and-blood lover ever saw.

But for all that, in private life she was a loving, sentimental creature. A loyal and generous friend, and thoughtful. She forgot nothing: names, dates, obligations. These included Hollywood, the people and institutions who had helped to make and keep her a star. When it was fashionable to rail against the studio system and the tycoons who had built it, she was always warm in their defense. She spoke of Metro as a family, in which she was directed and protected, provided with good stories and just about every great male star to play opposite; later she built up a similar relationship with Warners. And through it all, she was constantly herself, unmistakably Joan Crawford.

Katharine Hepburn says that every big star has the talent to irritate. Joan Crawford had that: whether you liked her or did not like her on screen, you could not ignore her existence or deny her quality. I thought Joan Crawford could never die. Come to think of it, as long as celluloid holds together and the word Hollywood means anything to anyone, she never will.

1906 Born Lucille Fay LeSueur in San Antonio, to newly separated parents.

1916 The family moves to Kansas City, where Lucy works in the school she attends—waiting on students, washing dishes, and cooking.

1924 Vowing to be "the best dancer in the world," Lucy is plucked from a nightclub chorus to dance on Broadway. Seen by an MGM talent scout, she is signed to a $75/week contract and sets out for Hollywood—age 16.

1925 Reborn as "Joan Crawford," the winning entry in a Name a Movie Star magazine contest.

1928 With broad shoulders and blue eyes, Crawford rockets to fame in *Our Dancing Daughters*. Going on to make more than 80 movies, she becomes not just one of Hollywood's highest-paid actresses, but also the epitome of timeless, tireless glamour, exclaiming, "if you want to see the girl next door, go next door!"

1934 Meets her father for the first and last time when he visits the set of *Chained*.

1939 Plagued by miscarriages, Crawford adopts daughter Christina—the first of four adopted children—who later pens an acerbic account of her in *Mommy Dearest*, immortalizing the line "No more wire hangers!" and setting the stage for other lurid tell-alls.

1943 Tired of seeing the best roles go to Greta Garbo and Norma Shearer, Crawford asks MGM to drop her contract. Things go no better at Warner Bros. They pay her $500,000 for three pictures, but she rejects all scripts for two years straight.

1946 Wins the Academy Award for *Mildred Pierce*, but Crawford is beset by nerves, and stays home.

1955 After her three "dollhouse unions" to actors (Douglas Fairbanks, Jr.; Franchot Tone; and Phillip Terry) end in divorce, Crawford marries Alfred Steele, CEO of Pepsi, Inc. Revitalizing the company, Crawford flies to plant openings and hosts Pepsi parties in her plush Upper East Side Manhattan townhouse. When Steele dies four years later, she is elected to the board but continues to set a place for Steele at her dinner table.

1961 Tours to promote Pepsi, toting 15 trunks for up to 10 wardrobe changes a day.

1962 *Whatever Happened to Baby Jane?* debuts. Her on-set arguments with Bette Davis are legendary: Davis stocks the soda machines with Coke. Crawford retaliates by filling her pocket with rocks for a wrestling scene. After *Baby Jane*, she tenaciously hangs onto stardom in a number of thrillers and TV dramas—reveling in the attention of mostly female fans and responding with handwritten notes and gifts. "I love a hundred people clutching at my coat, clamoring for autographs."

1969 Teaches Steven Spielberg to belch while filming an episode of *Night Gallery*.

1977 Dies in her Manhattan townhouse, of a heart attack, age 71—a chorine and waitress who, with determination and discipline, became one of the great movie stars. "Send me flowers while I'm still alive," she once implored. "They won't do me a damn bit of good when I'm dead."

JAMES MASON

By Nicholas Meyer, colleague and friend

WRITTEN IN COMMEMORATION

I first made the acquaintance of James Mason when I was ten years old and my father introduced me to Jules Verne via the Walt Disney version of *20,000 Leagues Under the Sea*. Mason played the tragic Captain Nemo, master of the submarine *Nautilus*. It was a memorable encounter in which I not only became a rabid Jules Verne fan, but also fell in love with James Mason.

20,000 Leagues Under the Sea exercised a powerful hold on my imagination. I must have seen the film thirty times as a child (my best friend's mother would park us in the theater for safe-keeping all day), only half understanding its brooding, pessimistic over-tones—so utterly uncharacteristic of Disney fare—but fascinated by the dreamy wonders of the enchanted world below the surface of the waves. I think I wanted to live aboard the *Nautilus,* which struck me as an ideal home.

But in particular the haunted, driven persona of Captain Nemo as inhabited by James Mason—"played" is somehow an insufficient description of what he did with the role—seized hold of my fancy to such an extent that I even learned to play the Bach "Toccata in D minor" in a piano transcription (which is more, I daresay, than Mason did when he is seen playing the piece on the organ aboard the *Nautilus*). Later, when I read Verne's novel and his description of Nemo, only one face would ever spring to my mind to correspond to the Captain's dark, too-far-apart eyes. The tortured, guilt-laden performance, like so much of Mason's work, seems only to improve and acquire new subtleties with the passage of time. I can't tell whose idea it was to let us see the dying Nemo's hand reach up and for the last time open the *Nautilus's* irislike window on the world beneath the sea, but it is so delicate yet theatrical a touch that it would make sense to learn that it was Mason's. How interesting and how satisfying that he remembered playing Nemo as his pleasantest experience in Hollywood.

He was a delicate artist, James Mason, whose art was only slightly less self-effacing than that of the incomparable Guinness, but much more so than the bravura Olivier. His private life compelled none of the ghoulish fascination that has made lesser actors more talked about in supermarket checkout lines.

He was simply there, year in and year out, turning in performance after performance in all manner of films—great, good, indifferent—always worthy of his material and frequently much better, inexorably accumulating a body of work that ranks among filmdom's greatest achievements. He rarely wore makeup or changed his voice, that unique Yorkshire brogue (the world is not crowded with James Mason impersonators). A mustache or beard was as close as he came to disguising his features. His ability, notwithstanding these self-imposed restrictions, to wring himself from innumerable human portraits of stunning variety, can be likened to Tracy's or Bogart's: they did not pretend to be other people; they pretended other people were them.

He excelled at tormented individuals, communicating spiritual anguish almost Conradian in its exquisite detail. The ultimate source of that anguish was not too hard to divine: it was always the knowledge, consciously or semiconsciously, of aloneness, of separation from the rest of humanity, the sensation at once curious, hideous, hypnotic, and melancholy of being apart, what Melville called an Isolato, a stranger in a strange land, at once part of the race of men yet at the same time utterly removed from them. If we wondered at Masons' capacity to evoke an identification, it was wonder based on his uncanny genius for mirroring the paradox each of us feels in his soul—that of aloneness and loneliness in the midst of togetherness. It is this to which we respond so keenly in Mason's work, as witness the durability of such "outsiders" as Johnny McQueen (his favorite role), or Brutus, Norman Maine, or Humbert Humbert, or—and especially—Nemo.

Whether it was Mason's art or Mason himself projecting that splendid and pathetic duality seems hairsplitting and hardly the point, but whatever its origin, it infused his work with a connective tissue of memorable melancholy.

It must be said, as well, that he was a deft comedian, as anyone who screens *A Touch of Larceny* or *Gregory's Girl* will rediscover—though even in his comic roles that melancholy reminder of "otherness," of not quite being a part of whatever else is going on around him, is apparent.

And of course, he was a great villain, Dostoyevskian at times, suave, brutal, doomed, and above all, intelligent, self-knowing.

It was Mason's intelligence, his palpable wit in the Elizabethan sense, that informed all his portrayals and endowed each of them with a particular emphasis. If he was alienated in each role, it was his prodigious intellect in each character he played, thus providing his repertoire with endless variety. He was that rare performer who actually makes you believe he is not only feeling, but thinking.

Perhaps he was too subtle, or, unlike Guinness, did not have the good fortune to find his way into a popular epic like *Star Wars* and into the mass consciousness of a new generation.

On second thought, perhaps it's no accident that such a thing failed to come to pass. Mason was here, quietly perfect, eloquent, articulate about those deepest, most perplexing nooks in the human heart.

And now—again quietly—he is gone, but leaving behind a legacy of luminous humanity to inspire us all and to tell us there's beautiful things in the world.

1909 Born the son of a textile merchant in Huddersfield, England.

1927 At Cambridge, on a lark, discovers his taste for acting and abandons dream of becoming an architect.

1935 His first film role is a reporter in *Late Extra*, but the following years are spent in "quota quickies"—England's home-grown B pictures. Quickly carves out a niche for himself as a charismatic actor with a touch of menace.

1939 Shoots his own movie, *I Met a Murderer*, with two friends—a crime story in which Mason is the title murderer. Marries coproducer Pamela Kellino two years later.

1942 A conscientious objector, Mason refuses to do military service—causing a long-lasting rift with his family. But his career takes off with a series of melodramas in which he perfects the suave villain. *The Seventh Veil* is his breakthrough film, catapulting Mason to Britain's top box-office star. Disillusioned with the quality of films he is offered, he decamps for Hollywood at the pinnacle of his popularity.

1947 His first Broadway outing, *Bathsheba,* is unsuccessful.

1954 After waiting several years for a plum movie, he lands *A Star Is Born* opposite Judy Garland—delivering a harrowing performance of a man in decline, and netting an Oscar nomination. (Mason doesn't like the film and doesn't show up at the Academy Awards, explaining, "The Oscar show is always a little better when things go wrong, so I had no need to feel guilty about letting them down.") Bringing the same nervous intensity to his subsequent roles, he makes a reputation in roles calling for moody introspection: Brutus *(Julius Ceasar),* Flaubert *(Madame Bovary),* and Captain Nemo *(20,000 Leagues Under the Sea.)*

1959 Menaces Cary Grant in *North by Northwest,* setting the stage for colorful supporting roles.

1962 Plays Humbert Humbert in Kubrick's *Lolita,* conceivably his best role. Mason daringly elicits sympathy—and humor—for his middle-aged infatuation with a 12-year-old girl. Maintaining a prolific output for the '60s and '70s, he accepts roles that are not worthy of his talent, but succeeds in elevating poorer films and enriching the better ones. Unworthy credits pile up on his résumé.

1964 Divorces Pamela Kellino.

1971 Marries second wife, Clarissa Kaye, an Australian actress.

1981 Publishes autobiography, *Before I Forget.*

1984 Dies in Lausanne, Switzerland, at 75—an actor of more than 100 movies, with a mellifluous voice and uncanny ability to suggest rampant emotion beneath a face of absolute calm. On his reputation: "I'm a character actor: the public never knows what it's getting by way of a Mason performance from one film to the next. I therefore represent thoroughly insecure investment."

GREGORY PECK

By Larry Gelbart, friend and poker buddy

DELIVERED AT MEMORIAL SERVICE, OCTOBER 20, 2003
THE ACADEMY OF MOTION PICTURE ARTS AND SCIENCES, LOS ANGELES

For openers, he had the kind of face that belonged on money. He really couldn't be more handsome if he tried. And the beauty of his beauty was that Greg never had to try at all. Add to that, an inner posture—an internal gyroscope that served him, and us, so well.

It would be a disservice, though, if we failed to note just how much fun the man could be. His *Paradine Case* costar and long-time friend, Louis Jourdan, put it best when he said about Greg: "He can be funny, which is fortunate. Otherwise such perfection would be unbearable."

Greg's sense of humor was one spiked with gusto. And a keen

appetite for adventure. Nothing delighted him more than treating his friends to a tear down a mountainside in Vail or Aspen. You have no absolutely no idea what it's like to look over and see Abraham Lincoln go whizzing by you at seventy-five miles an hour on a snowmobile.

Although not completely whizzing by. One of Greg's favorite tricks was—on catching up to you—to lean over and push the kill button on the engine of your machine.

In St. Moritz, Art Buchwald dared Greg to luge down the steep, murderous Cresta Run. It was the kind of dare that Greg couldn't resist. In a flash—no stand-in, no stunt man—suddenly, Captain Ahab, Captain Horatio Hornblower, and Captain Newman, M.D., immediately turned into Captain Marvel—and Greg went knifing across the ice under a wintry sky.

And with the same—literally flat-out—commitment that he showed marching under the hot sun with Martin Luther King. Imbued with the same sense of pride he felt learning he'd been named a Kennedy Center Honoree as he was earning the distinction of being on Nixon's Enemies List.

First, always, on Greg's list—first, always was the woman who was his source of endless delight. The woman who made the Peck home seem like a constantly refreshed flower vase. Veronique, his loving accomplice, and coconspirator in their countless string of what Greg called their "excellent adventures." The most excellent one being their own union.

On a visit to New York in 1980, Greg had an inspiration: On the spur of the moment, they flew by Concorde to Paris, arriving in time to attend Mass at Notre Dame. After which, he and Veronique made a U-turn, took another Concorde, and were back in New York in time to celebrate Mass at St. Patrick's Cathedral.

It was with that same sort of spontaneity, mixed with a touch of

Peckian mischief, that Greg, on another visit to New York, arranged an evening's entertainment that consisted of:

Attending a concert of another lifelong buddy, Frank Sinatra, at Lincoln Center.

Hustling over to Michael's Pub, in time to see Mel Torme perform.

Then, for the musical cherry on top, catching Joe Williams's last set at yet another jazz club.

As catholic in his tastes as he was in his faith, Greg was as turned on by Tina Turner as he was by Mozart. As much at home with Count Tolstoy as he was with Count Basie.

The New York City that was Peck Central for jazz sets and jet setting was a far cry from the New York City that greeted the ex-premed student, who stepped off the train there in 1939, and, with what was to prove to be his characteristic fortitude already locked in place, became an acting student at Sanford Meisner's prestigious Neighborhood Playhouse. Having been given only an acting, and not an eating, scholarship—in order to keep his body at the same level as his soul—Greg found himself working as (among other things):

A guide at Rockefeller Center.
A barker at New York's World's Fair.
A model for magazines, and for the pages of the Montgomery Ward catalog.

Can you believe there ever really was a time when you could rent Gregory Peck for five dollars an hour?

He waited tables, of course. That's a given.

When he was not flush enough to order nine-cent breakfasts at Nedick's, he'd sleep in Central Park, where a meal for him would often consist of the contents of a box of pancake mix.

As hungry for success as he was just plain hungry—ready to

leap, if not pole vault at each and any opportunity—Greg just happened to be standing next to the Neighborhood Playhouse's office receptionist, just as she just happened to be on the phone with the famed Broadway director Guthrie McClintock.

Having seen Greg in a Playhouse production, McClintock wondered if he might be interested in playing a small role in one of the director's upcoming productions on Broadway. Knowing exactly where the man's office was, Greg tore away from the receptionist, fairly flew down four flights of stairs, raced half a block across 46th Street, scurried four blocks up Sixth Avenue, and dashed into the lobby of the RKO Building at 50th. Sweating out what felt like a slow elevator to China, Greg got off on the eighth floor, and burst into McClintock's office—where the director was still talking on the phone with the receptionist at the Neighborhood Playhouse about the possibility of hiring Greg.

Seeing the gangly, completely winded young man standing in his doorway, Greg later reported, McClintock laughed so hard, he slid out of his chair and fell to the floor.

If you don't know whether or not Greg landed the job, you are definitely in the wrong building.

It was during this time, this fledgling period, that the twenty-four-year-old acting student/waiter/barker/guide/model/ and Aunt Jemima gourmand, Gregory Peck, wrote the following to his father—the man who had so hoped that his son would give up his foolish ideas and become a doctor.

"Two years is little enough to spend learning my craft, even though I may be letting a few $40 weekly jobs go by the boards," Greg wrote. "There will be no limit for me in a few years, and I assure you that, by 1943, you will have the best answer in the world to anyone who thinks your son is crazy today—an answer in lights."

He was off by only one year.

In 1944, he made his first two motion pictures: *Days of Glory* followed by *Keys of the Kingdom*.

In 1945, theater marquees were reading: INGRID BERGMAN AND GREGORY PECK STARRING IN *SPELLBOUND*.

My journey from fan to friend started pretty much around this period. My father was a barber in Beverly Hills, with a colorful assortment of clients. Celebrities that ranged from David O. Selznick to Bugsy Siegel. Even more improbably: from President Kennedy to Jack Ruby.

It was in my father's workplace where I, as a teenager, got to meet stars like Kirk Douglas and Gregory Peck—never dreaming that, half a century later, I'd find myself as part of a weekly poker group that included that very same Kirk Douglas. That very same Gregory Peck.

Me—sitting across the poker table from Spartacus and Atticus.

To say nothing of the never-ever-to-be-forgotten Jack Lemmon, as well.

It was in these games that I got to—up close—experience the honey-soaked, mellifluous quality of Greg's voice. See what a performance a superb actor can give, while bluffing with only a pair of twos. I discovered how salty his speech could be. And how peppered with literary references.

And just how perceptive a reader of other people he was.

Honing in on an aspect of my wife, Pat's, personality, Greg renamed her "Peaches." It was an apt and insightful act and a rechristening that has stuck to this day.

I learned first-hand, playing—and working with Greg as a coproducer of an Academy Awards show—that in an industry where one is all too often aware of the tiny patter of clay feet, no one ever had to wonder what Gregory Peck meant by what he said.

Gregory Peck always said exactly what he meant.

Some years ago, he told an interviewer that he considered himself a damn lucky man. I would only add that Greg most certainly earned every bit of luck that came his way. And that luck obviously recognized a man worthy of its favor when it saw one.

I know that those of us who are privileged to carry his memory with us are just as damn lucky. Lucky to have been rewarded with that sweetest of keepsakes.

1916 Born in La Jolla, California. His father is "Doc Peck," town pharmacist, who imbues him with small-town values and a bucolic childhood: one-room schoolhouse, beloved dog, July 4 parades down Main Street.

1925 Gregory is sent to live with his grandmother, who takes him to the movies regularly.

1938 Graduating from Berkeley, Peck heads for NYC, where he debuts on Broadway in *The Morning Star*. The play is undistinguished, but Peck wins good reviews. Supports himself as an NBC tour guide and catalog model for Montgomery Ward.

1944 Catapults to film stardom: His role in *The Keys of the Kingdom* hints at his trademark-to-be, morally anguished heroes showing courage under pressure, and nets him an Oscar nomination. The following year, Peck is nominated again, for Hitchcock's *Spellbound*. With eligible leading men in short supply, his stock soars in Hollywood; when he turns down a contract at MGM, Peck reduces studio head Louis B. Mayer to tears.

1946 Takes a holiday from decency, playing murderous son in *Duel in the Sun*. Disparaged by critics, the film is still a hit.

1953 Filming *Roman Holiday* with Audrey Hepburn, Peck is privately depressed about his recent separation from his first wife—but meets and later marries journalist Veronique Passani. When she tells him about passing up an interview with Albert Schweitzer to go on a date with Peck, he replies, "You made the right choice, kiddo!"

1962 Finally wins an Oscar, for *To Kill a Mockingbird*, his most celebrated role and personal favorite. Atticus Finch is later voted "greatest screen hero" by the AFI, beating out Indiana Jones and James Bond. On Atticus: "I put everything I had into it, everything I'd learned in 46 years of living, and my feelings about racial injustice and inequality."

1967 Receives the Academy's Humanitarian Award. An activist, Peck's ennobled roles make him a persuasive advocate for his causes: chairman, American Film Institute; chairman, American Cancer Society; president, Academy of Motion Picture Arts and Sciences; charter member, National Council on the Arts.

1968 As president of the Academy—and frequent marcher for civil rights—Peck postpones the Oscars when Martin Luther King is assassinated.

1969 Receives the nation's highest civilian award, Presidential Medal of Freedom.

1976 Takes a role in *The Omen* for $250,000—a huge salary cut, in exchange for 10% of the take. When the film goes on to gross $60 million in the U.S., Peck gets the largest paycheck of his career. Four years later, worried about the 600,000 auto jobs hanging on Chrysler's survival, he volunteers to become unpaid TV spokesman for the auto.

1982 Finding little to attract him in the '80s, he launches television career as Lincoln in *The Blue and the Gray* miniseries.

1989 Receives AFI's Lifetime Achievement Award.

2003 Dies, age 87, at his home in Los Angeles. Survived by his wife and four children, the fundamentally decent hero with chiseled looks once offered this explanation on his choice of roles: "I don't think I could stay interested for a couple of months in a character of mean motivation."

TALLULAH BANKHEAD

By Anita Loos, close friend and screenwriter

DELIVERED AT MEMORIAL SERVICE, DECEMBER 16, 1968
ST. JOHN THE DIVINE CATHEDRAL, NEW YORK CITY

It was my privilege to meet Tallulah when she was about sixteen and just arrived in New York from Alabama, possessed by the idea of being an actress. She was chaperoned by her beloved Aunt Marie, who was in utter accord with Tallulah's ambitions but remained so discreetly in the background that today I can't remember ever seeing her.

Tallulah's advent in New York bore a curious aura of Destiny. She and Aunt Marie knew nothing at all about life in the big city but, when they left the station bent on finding an economical place to live, Fate unaccountably led them to West Forty-fourth Street, where they were attracted by two smallish hotels. One was the Algonquin, which was even more a hotbed of theatrical life than it is today. Tallulah and Aunt Marie stood on the sidewalk between the Algonquin and the ultradecorous Seymour, hesitating over a choice. On the surface there seemed no difference between the two places, but finally, for a reason that could only have been mystical, they entered the Algonquin. It was as if Alice had walked smack into Wonderland without having to go down the Rabbit Hole. For on Tallulah's first day in New York, she was under the same roof with the aristocracy of the New York theater, among them Ethel Barrymore, her brother Jack, their uncle John Drew, Elsie Janis, and numberless others. And there were always a few important film people at the Algonquin, on leave from Hollywood. At the time, Constance Talmadge and Conway Tearle had come on to film a movie script of mine *(The Virtuous Vamp)* and I was with them.

Tallulah had no definite scheme to back up her overweening ambition, no letters of introduction or the least bit of schooling for the career she had chosen. Her first move was merely to take up a post in the hotel lobby where she could sit and gaze, entranced, at the comings and goings of the show folks. But Tallulah's blonde beauty was so dazzling that in no time at all, the show folks began to gaze at her. And, never known for her reticence, Tallulah was quite easy to contact. One of the first to whom she confided her acting ambitions was our director, John Emerson, who forthwith gave her a role as an extra in our movie. So my friendship with Tallulah began at the very beginning of her fantastic career.

Tallulah was so exhilarated by life in the ramshackle old studio in the East Fifties where we worked that, at first, we put her down as a run-of-the-mill movie fan. And we all considered her far too pretty to be anything but stupid. It wasn't long before we were set right on that score and alerted to the fact that our little Southern belle was to become one of the great wits of an entire era.

In those days the Algonquin dining rooms served as a showcase for a self-glorifying group of exhibitionists who termed their daily sessions the Round Table. Its leader was the critic Alec Woollcott, who greatly enjoyed his privileges of leadership, and one day granted the unsophisticated little blonde the special favor of attending one of those feasts of reason and flows of soul. Tallulah listened demurely as the group sat about, self-consciously cueing each other and quoting themselves, at the end of which, she turned to Alec and, in the throaty tones that were so fully developed at sixteen, spoke her mind. "Mr. Woollcot," said Tallulah, "there is less here than meets the eye." From that moment on, Alec pursued Tallulah, but whether it was out of masochism, or through fear of comments she might make if he were *not* present, is a moot question.

With her unerring sense of values, Tallulah selected only the right people as friends from among the Algonquin set; she became a welcome satellite of Ethel Barrymore, who delighted in advising her about her career. But when that great lady of the theatre informed Tallulah that her outlandish name would work against her in show business and advised that she call herself Barbara, Tallulah refused to listen. She knew by instinct that no other name would ever express her turgid but sericomic, nature; Tallulah's basic essence was too strong to be diluted even by Ethel Barrymore. "Tallulah" she must always be—doubtless the most properly named character ever to tread the boards.

Utterly contemptuous of phonies and anything but a self-deceiver, Tallulah never believed the middle-class theory that ambition is praiseworthy. She saw it for what it generally is, a matter of conceit mixed, more or less, with cupidity. And so Tallulah never allowed ambition to interfere with play. She lived in the grand manner of a free soul with an aristocratic disdain for caution. And although many of her impulses were unfortunate, none harmed anybody but herself; the great majority of them came straight from her enormous interest in others, her kindness and unfailing courtesy toward anyone who deserved it. Heaven help anyone who didn't; although in such cases there is evidence that Heaven generally took sides with Tallulah. Among the humble and unpretentious, she behaved with the discretion and impeccable manners of a very great lady.

During the days of the silent films in Hollywood, we both lived at the old Hollywood Hotel. Although it had been largely taken over by the movie contingent, there were also a number of old people from the Middle West living there in retirement. They were as truly nice as they were boring, and none of us girls who worked in films ever bothered to give them the time of day as they sat rocking their afternoons away on the front porch. But Tallulah did. And I still carry a picture in my memory of her sitting on the porch of the hotel and allowing an old lady from Iowa to teach her a crochet stitch. Tallulah, with no intention of ever crocheting anything, at any time, pretended an interest out of kindness and as a means of communication. "You can say all you want about the wickedness of film stars," the old lady said to me, "but that little Bankhead girl is as sweet and unspoiled as if she lived in Des Moines!"

Later on, when the talkies came in, I had a house in Santa Monica, where Tallulah, on afternoons when she was free from work, used to come to swim in my pool. While it may be difficult today to realize there used to be a convention against taking off one's clothes in public, Tallulah like all great souls was ahead of her time; she never had any more need of a bathing suit than a dolphin. Now it so happened that next door to me there was a construction crew building a house, and while Tallulah cavorted in the pool, the crew would knock off work and mount a scaffolding to watch. I happened to be busy in the studio at the time, and the first I heard of Tallulah's gambols was when the owner of the new house called up to tell me that work had fallen alarmingly behind schedule, and he pleaded that I ask Tallulah to put on a bathing suit and let his builders get back on the job. Heedful that their work stoppage was creating a deficit, Tallulah promptly complied.

There was a time in London when a beautiful and quite scandalous queen of a Graustarkian kingdom of Central Europe was causing alarm in orthodox royal circles. None of those royalties came to her rescue. She took HRH in as a houseguest, and I remember one evening when a card game was projected that Tallulah whispered instruction of all of us to play stupidly and allow Her Highness to clean up. "She's flat broke," explained our hostess, "and trying to support the most divine young gigolo."

Living a life of high celebrity, Tallulah took just as much interest in unfortunates as she did in the famous. During part of her career in New York, Tallulah was beset by insomnia and, unable to sleep, spent her nights listening to a radio broadcaster who went by the name of Big Joe. Big Joe's program consisted of interviews with down-and-outers, whose dire situations provided him with fascinating material. Listening to Big Joe, Tallulah's heart and pocketbook never failed to respond. And before very long the program became a two-way broadcast with Tallulah on the phone exchanging comments and bits of homespun philosophy with Big Joe and his assorted vagrants. But Tallulah could spot a phony, even across the airways and, as a rule, it was the most unregenerate scamps who told the truth about themselves and to whom Tallulah was the most responsive. On a cold winter night she sent for an utterly dissolute young woman and gave her one of her most expensive fur coats.

Never at a loss for the mot juste, Tallulah could match wits with experts such as Winston Churchill and come out even. And incidentally, Tallulah could also match the prime minister's alcoholic capacity, drink for drink. When tight she might become outrageous, but Tallulah never bored anyone, and *that* I consider to be humanitarianism of a very high order indeed.

1902 Born in Huntsville, Ala. Tallulah is sent to live with relatives after her mother dies from complications from childbirth. Her father, U.S. Congressman William Bankhead, is devastated.

1917 Wins a movie-magazine beauty contest and moves to NYC. She is 15.

1920 Becomes a peripheral member of the Algonquin Roundtable—known for her biting wit, hard-partying ways, and love affairs with both men and women. "My father warned me about men and booze. But he never mentioned a word about women and cocaine."

1923 After years of middling success in New York, Tallulah makes her debut on London's West End —to the immediate adoration of critics and fans. She stays for eight years, appearing in 24 plays and becoming one of England's best-known actresses. Away from the prying eyes of her family, Tallulah becomes wilder. "I've tried several varieties of sex. The conventional position makes me claustrophobic. And the others give me either stiff neck or lockjaw."

1931 Returns to the U.S. to be Paramount's newest sex goddess, but critics find her acting flat—and consider her outclassed by Marlene Dietrich and Carole Lombard. She returns to Broadway.

1937 Marries actor John Emery. The marriage is largely to placate her father, who was Speaker of the House. Four years later, they divorce.

1939 Wows Broadway in *The Little Foxes*, her first American stage triumph. Receiving unanimous praise and 10% of the grosses, Tallulah stays with the play for 408 performances.

1944 Hitchcock casts her in *Lifeboat*, her best screen performance.

1950 Retires from the stage to host an NBC radio show. *The Big Show* is a smash, due in part to Tallulah's trademark wit. (Tallulah to Ethel Merman: "I must say, dahling, you don't look a day over sixty!") She publishes her autobiography, which spends 26 weeks on the *New York Times* bestseller list.

1957 Appears on the *Lucy* (Lucille Ball) TV show as the "celebrity next door"—drunk. The years of 100 cigarettes and two bottles of Old Grand Dad per day take their toll. Job offers dwindle. She becomes a homebody, retreating to her New York apartment.

1968 Dies of pneumonia. Her last discernible words are "codeine" and "bourbon." "If I had my life to live over again, I'd make the same mistakes, only sooner."

ORSON WELLES

By Charlton Heston, colleague and admirer

DELIVERED AT MEMORIAL SERVICE, NOVEMBER 2, 1985
THE DIRECTORS' GUILD, LOS ANGELES

One of the luckiest things that ever happened to me in my career, I think, was the chance to work with Orson Welles in *A Touch of Evil.* It was an extraordinary experience, and an enormously valuable lesson in film. He taught me all kinds of things: how important it is for actors with bass voices to use their tenor range. He was the first man to ever take me into a cutting room, which he did with great generosity and patience.

He also was the most entertaining director I've ever worked for. People imagine filmmaking is a lot of fun. "Oh it must have been marvelous fun to work with so and so, to do that, to be there." Not true. Filmmaking is very hard work, long days filled with frustration and failure on every hand. You often face a bitter truth: to see yourself falling a little short.

With Orson, somehow, this was not so. It was always exciting—almost a party. "Celebration" is better—it was a celebration. Many of the shots are just structural shots, but Orson could persuade you that a shot where you drove up and got out of a car and went up a flight of stairs and in a door just happened to be the most important shot in the entire film.

I don't know if he was the best director that ever lived. I suppose he wasn't the best actor. He was an enormously gifted writer, director, producer. I do know that he was the most talented man I ever worked with. Talent is a slippery word in itself—it's that smoky something hidden somewhere inside us allowing us to make up plays and paintings and bridges and airplanes and murals—and movies. Orson had more of that than anyone I've ever known.

Indeed, he was so enormously gifted that things came from him casually, quite often under pressure—sudden leaps of the imagination, of creative intelligence, in moments of absolute pain—that I think that unconsciously he may have created these situations. He painted himself into corners just to see how he could get out of them. This, of course, created a sense of wary skepticism in those for whom he worked. And especially in those to whom he had to turn for money. Unhappily, Orson always denied the basic fact of filmmaking: that the raw materials are so expensive that we cannot afford to buy them for ourselves; we must get them from people who have the money, and they want it back; and that's fair.

The only people Orson would never bother to charm (and he could charm anyone) were studio heads. The people who have the money. Which is one of the reasons we have so few pictures from him. We have what is arguably the greatest picture of all, *Citizen Kane*. And Cahier du Cinema described *A Touch of Evil* as "the best 'B' movie ever made." That is itself a reflection of the ambiguous skepticism with which the film community regarded Orson. But we're lucky to have the films we have; it is our grievous loss that we haven't more of them.

As epitaph, I want to speak a few words from a play we both did many times, *Julius Caesar*. I played Antony, he played Brutus—to my great loss, never together. But it speaks to some of things I feel.

> He was my friend, faithful and just to me,
> but Brutus says he was ambitious.
> If it were so, it were a grievous fault
> and grievously hath Caesar answered it.
> He was the noblest Roman of them all,
> the elements so mixed in him that nature
> must stand up and say to all the world,
> "This was a man."

1915 Born to an inventor and a beautiful concert pianist.

1924 His mother dies, and Orson travels the world with his bon vivant father. When his father dies six years later, he is adopted by his physician, Dr. Bernstein, who declares him a prodigy and furnishes him with gifts—including a violin, a magic set, and a theatrical makeup kit.

1930 Touring Ireland, he convinces a Dublin theater manager that he's an actor on holiday and goes on in several featured roles.

1934 A packed year: Joining the prestigious Katherine Cornell theater company, Welles debuts on Broadway as Tybalt. "He has the manner of a giant with the look of a child, a mad wisdom, and a solitude encompassing the world," Jean Cocteau says of the 19-year-old. Also gets married, debuts on the radio, and makes his first short film.

1937 Directs a theatrical production of *Julius Caesar,* switching the setting to Fascist Rome. Follows up with an all-black *Macbeth*.

1938 Produces *The War of the Worlds* on radio. Depicting a Martian invasion with eyewitness accounts and news bulletins, the show scares the bejeezus out of listeners and roots Welles's name in pop culture. Welles and CBS are flooded with lawsuits, all dismissed, and the episode becomes a textbook case for mass hysteria.

1941 Hollywood calls: The 25-year-old Welles is offered an unprecedented "final cut" on his first feature by RKO Pictures. *Citizen Kane* loses $150,000 for RKO, but is regarded by many as the best movie ever made—boldly offering new narrative techniques, camerawork, special effects, even makeup, as Welles ages several decades. His theatrical background is in full evidence: Welles stacks the film with long takes without close-ups. (Years later, when *Kane* is colorized, he bellows, "Keep Ted Turner and his Crayolas away from my movie!")

1942 His career takes a disastrous turn with *The Magnificent Ambersons*, which goes overbudget, is reedited by RKO, and seen by few. Welles gets a reputation as an irresponsible director and spendthrift. The film becomes a classic.

1943 Rejected by the army because of "flat feet," Welles tours Europe as a magician. His act consists of sawing Marlene Dietrich in half. Later that year, he marries Rita Hayworth—the second of three wives.

1948 A large man with an outsized appetite for food, cigars, and life, he decamps for Europe after a string of commercial failures.

1958 Directs *A Touch of Evil*, one of the best B pictures ever made, starring (eulogizer) Charlton Heston. It fails in the U.S. Welles gains more weight, despite doctor's advice to "stop having intimate dinners for four, unless there are three other people."

1975 Welles receives the AFI's Lifetime Achievement Award.

1984 The Director's Guild bestows its highest honor, the D. W. Griffith Award.

1985 Dies of a heart attack, age 70, having created a movie classic, terrified hundreds of thousands of radio listeners, and changed the face of film and radio with daring new ideas. His ashes are buried in an old well of a Spanish bullfighter. Though he wrestled much of his life with unfulfilled promise, and was vilified by Hollywood, in the end few denied his genius. Marlene Dietrich: "People should cross themselves when they say his name."

PIONEERS

PRINCESS DIANA

By Lord Edward John Spencer, brother

DELIVERED AT FUNERAL, SEPTEMBER 6, 1997
WESTMINSTER ABBEY, LONDON

I stand before you today the representative of a family in grief, in a country in mourning, before a world in shock. We are all united, not only in our desire to pay our respects to Diana but rather in our need to do so. For such was her extraordinary appeal that the tens of millions of people taking part in this service all over the world via television and radio, who never actually met her, feel that they, too, lost someone close to them in the early hours of Sunday morning. It is a more remarkable tribute to Diana than I can ever hope to offer her today.

Diana was the very essence of compassion, of duty, of style, of beauty. All over the world she was a symbol of selfless humanity, a standard-bearer for the rights of the truly downtrodden, a very

British girl who transcended nationality, someone with a natural nobility who was classless and who proved in the last year that she needed no royal title to continue to generate her particular brand of magic.

Today is our chance to say thank you for the way you brightened our lives, even though God granted you but half a life. We will all feel cheated always that you were taken from us so young, and yet we must learn to be grateful that you came along at all. Only now that you are gone do we truly appreciate what we are now without, and we want you to know that life without you is very, very difficult. We have all despaired at our loss over the past week, and only the strength of the message you gave us through your years of giving has afforded us the strength to move forward.

There is a temptation to rush to canonize your memory. There is no need to do so; you stand tall enough as a human being of unique qualities not to need to be seen as a saint. Indeed, to sanctify your memory would be to miss out on the very core of your being—your wonderfully mischievous sense of humor with a laugh that bent you double, your joy for life transmitted wherever you took your smile and the sparkle in those unforgettable eyes, your boundless energy which you could barely contain. But your greatest gift was your intuition, and it was a gift you used wisely. That is what underpinned all your other wonderful attributes, and if we look to analyze what it was about you that had such a wide appeal, we find it in your instinctive feel for what was really important in our lives. Without your God-given sensitivity we would be immersed in greater ignorance of the anguish of AIDS and HIV sufferers, the plight of the homeless, the isolation of lepers, the random destruction of land mines.

Diana explained to me once that it was her innermost feelings of suffering that made it possible for her to connect with her constituency of the rejected. And here we come to another truth about her. For all the status, the glamour, the applause, Diana remained throughout a very insecure person at heart, almost childlike in her desire to do good for others so she could release herself from deep feelings of unworthiness of which her eating disorders were merely a symptom. The world sensed this part of her character and cherished her for her vulnerability whilst admiring her for her honesty.

The last time I saw Diana was on July the first, her birthday, in London, when, typically, she was not taking time to celebrate her special day with friends but was guest of honor at a fund-raising charity evening. She sparkled, of course, but I would rather cherish the days I spent with her in March when she came to visit me and my children in our home in South Africa. I am proud of the fact that, apart from when she was on public display meeting President Mandela, we managed to contrive to stop the ever-present paparazzi from getting a single picture of her. That meant a lot to her.

These were days I will always treasure. It was as if we had been transported back to our childhood when we spent such an enormous amount of time together, the two youngest in the family. Fundamentally, she hadn't changed at all from the big sister who mothered me as a baby, fought with me at school, and endured those long train journeys between our parents' homes with me at weekends. It is a tribute to her level-headedness and strength that, despite the most bizarre life imaginable after her childhood, she remained intact, true to herself.

There is no doubt that she was looking for a new direction in her life at this time. She talked endlessly of getting away from England, mainly because of the treatment that she received at the hands of newspapers. I don't think she ever understood why her genuinely good intentions were sneered at by the media, why there appeared to be a permanent quest on their behalf to bring her down. It is baffling. My own, and only, explanation is that genuine goodness is threatening to those at the opposite end of the moral spectrum. It is a point to remember that, of all the ironies about Diana, perhaps the greatest was this: A girl given the name of the ancient goddess of hunting was, in the end, the most hunted person of the modern age.

She would want us today to pledge ourselves to protecting her beloved boys, William and Harry, from a similar fate, and I do this here, Diana, on your behalf. We will not allow them to suffer the anguish that used regularly to drive you to tearful despair. And beyond that, on behalf of your mother and sisters, I pledge that we, your blood family, will do all we can to continue the imaginative and loving way in which you were steering these two exceptional young men so that their souls are not simply immersed by duty and tradition, but can sing openly as you planned. We fully respect the heritage into which they have both been born, and will always respect and encourage them in their royal role, but we, like you, recognize the need for them to experience as many different aspects of life as possible to arm them spiritually and emotionally for the years ahead. I know you would have expected nothing less from us.

William and Harry, we all care desperately for you today. We are all chewed up with sadness at the loss of a woman who wasn't even our mother. How great your suffering is, we cannot even imagine.

I would like to end by thanking God for the small mercies he has shown us at this dreadful time; for taking Diana at her most beautiful and radiant, and when she had joy in her private life. Above all, we give thanks for the life of a woman I am so proud to be able to call my sister—the unique, the complex, the extraordinary and irreplaceable Diana, whose beauty, both internal and external, will never be extinguished from our minds.

1961 Born Diana Frances Spencer—youngest daughter of the eighth Earl Spencer. When her parents divorce six years later, custody is awarded to her father.

1975 The family moves to Althorp, a stately house dating to 1508.

1977 Having failed her O-level exams, Diana leaves the prestigious West Heath School to attend a finishing school, where she becomes a talented pianist, excels in sports, and longs to become a ballerina—though she is so retiring as to accept only nonspeaking parts in school plays.

1978 Moves to London, where she works as a nanny, governess, and kindergarten teacher.

1981 Following an exhaustive search, and under intense pressure to take a bride, Prince Charles courts Diana—a stylish girl who met Buckingham Palace's rigid bridal requirements: (1) aristocratic background; (2) Protestant; (3) a virgin. The resulting wedding is a grand affair watched by 1 billion TV viewers. Draped in white silk taffeta with a 25-foot train, Diana is the first Englishwoman to marry an heir apparent to the throne since 1659—becoming Her Royal Highness the Princess of Wales. The fairy tale begins.

1982 And begins to disintegrate: After Prince William is born, Diana suffers postnatal depression—attempting suicide several times and starting her battle with eating disorders. She maintains appearances: To the outside world, the girl in maiden dresses with a bowl hairdo had been transformed into an elegant fashion plate whose every style is photographed, dissected, and reborn into the wardrobes of well-dressed women everywhere.

1984 Prince Harry is born.

1986 Her marriage unravels as publicly as it began. Charles resumes his relationship with prior girlfriend Camilla Parker Bowles. Diana becomes involved with several men—including her riding instructor—but eventually channels her grief into charity work, exclaiming, "Anywhere I see suffering, that is where I want to be, doing what I can." From here on out, she is pursued relentlessly by the tabloids.

1987 Sitting on the bed of an HIV victim and holding his hand, she becomes the first celebrity warrior against AIDS who touches a patient—working hard to change fear of the mysterious disease. "Don't call me an icon," she warns, "I'm only a mother trying to help." Subsequently tours landmine-strewn countries with the Red Cross. Although mine-clearance experts have already cleared the path, pictures of Diana touring a minefield in a ballistic helmet and flak jacket are broadcast worldwide. To rebukes from politicians that she is meddling in partisan affairs: "I am not a political figure. I am a humanitarian figure and I always will be."

1992 Her divorce is finalized. She loses her Royal Highness title but not her sense of humor: "They say that it is better to be poor and happy than rich and miserable, but how about a compromise, like moderately rich and just moody?"

1995 Gives an extraordinary interview to the BBC, admitting her bulimia and adultery, and suggesting that the Royal Family was uncaring. Her popularity only grows.

1997 Hurtling into the Pont de L'Alma tunnel in Paris with boyfriend Dodi Fayed, pursued by nine dogged French paparazzi, Diana's Mercedes crashes. As she lies dying, the photographers continue snapping pictures. Her passing is greeted with extraordinary public grief: Diana's funeral draws 3 million mourners and a worldwide TV audience. More than a million bouquets are left at her London home. At the funeral, Elton John performs a rewritten version of "Candle in the Wind." Buried at Althorp in the middle of a lake, the shy young society girl who became one of the world's most glamorous and attention-getting women is laid to rest, age 36.

ROSA PARKS

By President Bill Clinton

DELIVERED AT MEMORIAL, NOVEMBER 2, 2005
GREATER GRACE TEMPLE, DETROIT, MICHIGAN

The world knows of Rosa Parks because of a single simple act of dignity and courage that struck a lethal blow to the foundations of legal bigotry. But fifty years and twenty-nine days ago, when Rosa Parks refused to give up her seat to a white man in the South, where segregation extended even to the close confines of the city bus, she was just taking the next step on her own long road to freedom.

It began when she was just eleven, when she moved to Montgomery because there was no school that admitted African-Americans beyond the sixth grade in her little town of Pine Level, Alabama.

It continued when she was nineteen, when she married Raymond Parks, a strong NAACP member who worked for the defense of the Scottsboro boys.

At thirty, she joined the NAACP—one of the first women to do so. In the same year, she made her first attempt to register to vote. And this highly articulate, intelligent, literate woman was judged to have failed the literacy test. In fact, the authorities failed the humanity test.

That same year, she had a prophetic run-in with a bus driver, who threw her off the bus because she insisted on entering the front door. Black folks were supposed to get on at the back and pay there.

At thirty-three, she finally got to vote. They couldn't figure out how to flunk her the third time on the literacy test.

At forty-two, after attending a workshop on integration at the Highlander Folk School in Tennessee, she got on that bus with the same old driver and refused to give up her seat to a white man in a region where gentlemen are supposed to give up their seats to ladies.

Rosa Parks ignited the most significant social movement in modern American history to finish the work that spawned the Civil War and redeem the promise of the Thirteenth, Fourteenth, and Fifteenth Amendments.

For fifty more years, she moved beyond the bus, continuing her work on that promise.

It was my honor to present her with the Presidential Medal of Freedom and to join the leaders of Congress in presenting her with a Congressional Gold Medal. I remember well when she sat with Hillary in the box of the first family at the State of the Union Address in 1999, and how the entire Congress, Democrats and Republicans alike, rose as one to recognize that she had made us all better people in a better country.

When I first met Rosa Parks, I was reminded of what Abraham Lincoln said when he was introduced to Harriet Beecher Stowe, the author of *Uncle Tom's Cabin*. He said, "So this is the little lady who started the great war." This time, Rosa's war was fought by Martin Luther King's rules: civil disobedience, peaceful resistance. But a war nonetheless for one America in which the law of the land means the same thing for everybody.

Rosa Parks was small in stature with delicate features. But the passing years did nothing to dim the light that danced in her eyes, the kindness and strength you saw in her smile, or the dignity of her voice. To the end, she radiated that kind of grace and serenity that God specially gives to those who stand in the line of fire for freedom and touch even the hardest hearts.

I remember, as if it were yesterday, that fateful day fifty years ago. I was a nine-year-old southern white boy who rode a segregated bus every single day of my life. I sat in the front. Black folk sat in the back. When Rosa showed us that black folks didn't have to sit in the back anymore, two of my friends and I, who strongly approved of what she had done, decided we didn't have to sit in the front anymore.

It was just a tiny gesture by three ordinary kids. But that tiny gesture was repeated over and over again millions and millions of times in the hearts and minds of children, their parents, their grandparents, their great grandparents, proving that she did help to set us all free.

And that great civil rights song that Nina Simone did so well . . . at the end it says I wish that you knew how it feels to be me, then you'd see and agree that everyone should be free.

Now that our friend Rosa Parks has gone on to her just reward, now that she has gone home and left us behind, let us never forget that in that simple act and a lifetime of grace and dignity, she showed us every single day what it means to be free. She made us see and agree that everyone should be free.

God bless you, Rosa.

1913 Born Rosa Louise McCauley in rigidly segregated Tuskegee, Ala. Her
father works as a carpenter and her mother as a teacher, who home-
schools Rosa until age 11, when she is sent to Miss White's School
for Girls.

1932 Marries barber Raymond Parks.

1933 After dropping out to care for her ailing grandmother, Rosa earns her
high school diploma—at a time when fewer than 7% of blacks had
diplomas. Following the timeworn footsteps of other educated black
women, Rosa becomes a seamstress.

1942 Sets up a youth council for the local NAACP.

1943 Refusing to enter a bus from the back door, Parks sets the stage for her
act of civil disobedience—even as she remains dignified and unfailingly
polite. The fires of equality are stoked.

1955 Takes a famous bus ride. By chance, the driver is the same man who
forced her off the bus 12 years earlier. When he asks her to stand so that
a white man can be seated (there are three empty seats near her vacated
by other blacks), she refuses—an act of civil disobedience dangerous for
its time. Blacks have been jailed, even killed, for disobeying bus drivers. "If
you don't stand up, I'm going to call the police," the driver says. Parks: "You
may do that." For her act of defiance, Parks is arrested, convicted of violat-
ing segregation laws, and fined $14. But her case becomes a rallying cry
for Montgomery blacks, and they organize a bus boycott which lasts 13
months. The country is captivated. A 26-year-old preacher named Martin
Luther King, Jr., is incensed. And the civil rights movement is ignited.

1956 The Supreme Court outlaws segregation on buses.

1957 But the violence escalates—snipers fire into buses and Dr. King's home.
Sacked from her tailoring job and fed up with telephone death threats,
Rosa and Raymond move to Detroit, where she continues working as a
seamstress.

1965 Hired by Congressman John Conyers as an aide, Rosa stays for 23 years.

1977 Raymond dies.

1987 Parks founds the Rosa and Raymond Parks Institute for Self Development—educating youth about civil rights and continuing her quiet activism well into her eighth decade.

1992 Her autobiography, *Rosa Parks: My Story,* hits bookstores.

1994 Her last years are troubled: A 28-year-old man beats and robs Parks. She begins to suffer from dementia. Having trouble making the rent, Parks relies on support from a local church. But the accolades arrive: she is subsequently awarded the Presidential Medal of Freedom, the Congressional Gold Medal of Honor, and honorary degrees from more than 40 universities. Soft spoken, Parks is uncomfortable with her near canonization. "Children want to know if I was alive during slavery—they equate me with Harriet Tubman and Sojourner Truth and ask if I knew them."

2005 Dies, age 92—a black seamstress whose refusal to surrender her bus seat to a white man launched the modern civil rights movement and inspired generations of activists. Her funeral is attended by thousands, who sing "We Shall Overcome" as they file past her casket. Transported from Detroit to Montgomery to Washington, D.C., she becomes the first woman to lie in honor in the Capitol Rotunda. Reverend Jesse Jackson: "Her imprisonment opened the doors for our long journey to freedom."

MARTIN LUTHER KING, JR.

By Robert F. Kennedy

DELIVERED AT CAMPAIGN PIT STOP, APRIL 4, 1968
INDIANAPOLIS, INDIANA

I have bad news for you, for all of our fellow citizens, and people who love peace all over the world, and that is that Martin Luther King was shot and killed tonight.

Martin Luther King dedicated his life to love and to justice for his fellow human beings, and he died because of that effort.

In this difficult day, in this difficult time for the United States, it is perhaps well to ask what kind of a nation we are and what direction we want to move in. For those of you who are black— considering the evidence that white people were responsible—you can be filled with bitterness, with hatred, and a desire for revenge. We can move in that direction as a country, in great polarization—black people amongst black, white people amongst white, filled with hatred toward one another.

Or we can make an effort, as Martin Luther King did, to comprehend and to replace that violence, that stain of bloodshed that has spread across our land, with an effort to understand with compassion and love.

For those of you who are black and are tempted with hatred and distrust at the injustice of such an act, against all white people, I can only say that I feel in my own heart the same kind of feeling. I had a member of my family killed, but he was killed by a white man. But we have to make an effort in the United States, we have to make an effort to understand, to go beyond these rather difficult times.

My favorite poet was Aeschylus. He wrote: "In our sleep, pain which cannot forget falls drop by drop upon the heart until, in our own despair, against our will, comes wisdom through the awful grace of God."

What we need in the United States is not division; what we need in the United States is not hatred; what we need in the United States is not violence or lawlessness; but love and wisdom, and compassion toward one another, and a feeling of justice toward those who still suffer within our country, whether they be white or they be black.

So I shall ask you tonight to return home, to say a prayer for the family of Martin Luther King, that's true, but more importantly to say a prayer for our own country, which all of us love—a prayer for understanding and that compassion of which I spoke. We can do well in this country. We will have difficult times; we've had difficult times in the past; we will have difficult times in the future. It is not the end of violence; it is not the end of lawlessness; it is not the end of disorder.

But the vast majority of white people and the vast majority of black people in this country want to live together, want to improve the quality of our life, and want justice for all human beings who abide in our land.

Let us dedicate ourselves to what the Greeks wrote so many years ago: to tame the savageness of man and make gentle the life of this world. Let us dedicate ourselves to that, and say a prayer for our country and for our people.

1929 Born Michael Luther King in Atlanta, Ga., to a religious family headed by Rev. Martin Luther King, Sr. Later renamed after his father.

1943 Age 14, Martin wins a speaking contest sponsored by the Negro Elks Society. On the bus ride home, he is forced to relinquish his seat to a white person and stand for the duration of the 90-mile trip. Later recalls, "I don't think I've ever been so deeply angry in my life."

1948 Upon graduating from Morehouse College, King is admitted to the Crozer Theological Seminary in Chester, Pa., where he is ordained as a Baptist minister at age 19.

1953 Marries Coretta Scott. Four children follow.

1954 Moves to Montgomery, Ala., to preach at Dexter Avenue Church. Avoiding the religious emotionalism of gospel churches ("The shouting and stomping . . . it embarrassed me"), King views the church as an instrument of social change.

1955 Seamstress Rosa Parks refuses to relinquish her bus seat to a white man in Montgomery. King leads a boycott of Montgomery buses. The civil rights movement begins.

1957 Delivers 208 speeches, developing exceptional oratorical skills.

1958 Publishes his first book, *Stride Toward Freedom,* an account of the Montgomery bus boycott. While promoting his book in a Harlem bookstore, King is stabbed by an African-American woman.

1959 Visits India to study Mahatma Gandhi's methods of nonviolent protest. Upon his return, King resigns from Dexter Avenue Church to focus on civil rights full-time. "Get the weapon of nonviolence, the breastplate of righteousness, the armor of truth," he tells his demonstrators in Alabama, "and just keep marching."

1960 King family moves to Atlanta, where King and his father become copastors of Ebenezer Baptist Church.

1963 Jailed (for the 13th time) during a march in Birmingham, Ala., a burgeoning battleground for civil rights. In jail, King writes *Letter from a Birmingham Jail,* asserting civilians have a moral duty to disobey unjust laws. *Letter* becomes a civil rights classic. Later that year, delivers his "I Have a Dream" speech at civil rights demonstration in Washington.

1964 Receives Nobel Peace Prize at age 35—the youngest recipient ever. Although he has been stabbed, physically attacked, and had his house bombed three times, King remains resolutely committed to nonviolence.

1968 Marches in support of sanitation workers in Memphis. Delivers his last speech, "I've Been to the Mountaintop." The next day, he is shot and killed at the Lorraine Hotel in Memphis by petty criminal James Earl Ray. His coffin is taken to the funeral atop a farm wagon pulled by two mules, in recognition of King's association with the poor. Despite pleas for nonviolence, there are resulting riots and disturbances in 130 American cities, and 20,000 arrests.

1986 The third Monday in January is proclaimed a holiday in King's honor.

CORETTA SCOTT KING

By President Jimmy Carter, friend

DELIVERED AT FUNERAL, FEBRUARY 7, 2006
NEW BIRTH MISSIONARY BAPTIST CHURCH, LITHONIA, GEORGIA

Since we left the White House, my wife and I have visited more than 125 nations in the world. They've been mostly nations where people are suffering; almost forty-five of them are in Africa. And we have found in those countries a remarkable gratitude for what Martin and Coretta have meant to them no matter where they live.

It's interesting for us Americans to realize that we do not have a monopoly on a hunger for democracy and freedom. We'll soon be going back to India—the largest democracy on earth—which is a Hindu nation. My wife and I have helped to have democratic elections in Indonesia, the fourth largest nation on earth, the largest Muslim country in the world, committed now to democracy.

And, of course, we have a country here with a diversity of religions—predominantly Christian—which is also a democracy. So we don't have a monopoly on achieving the greatest aspects of human nature.

It's not easy for us to realize the essence of human ambitions that bind us all together in all those countries in the world that admired the King family and what they meant.

Coretta and Martin and their family have been able to climb the highest mountain and to realize the essence of theology and political science and philosophy. They overcame one of the greatest challenges of life, which is to be able to wage a fierce struggle for freedom and justice and to do it peacefully.

It is always a temptation to forget that we worship the prince of peace.

Martin and Coretta demonstrated to the world that this correlation was possible. They exemplified the finest aspects of American values and brought upon our nation the admiration of the entire world.

This beautiful and brave woman helped to inspire her husband, has been a worthy successor in carrying forward his great legacy. They led a successful battle to alleviate the suffering of blacks and other minorities in promoting human rights. In promoting civil rights in our own country, they enhanced human rights in all nations.

And at the same time, they transformed the relationships among us Americans, breaking down the racial barriers that have separated us one from another for almost two centuries.

My life has been closely intertwined with that of the King family. Our first ceremony together was in 1974, when as governor I dedicated Martin's portrait in the Georgia Capitol, which was surrounded outside with chanting members of the Ku Klux Klan, who had too much support from other Americans.

The efforts of Martin and Coretta have changed America. They were not appreciated even at the highest level of government. It was difficult for them personally—with the civil liberties of both husband and wife violated as they became the target of secret government wiretapping, other surveillance, and as you know, harassment from the FBI.

When Coretta and Daddy King adopted me in 1976, it legitimized a southern governor as an acceptable candidate for president. Each of their public handshakes to me was worth a million Yankee votes.

In return, they had a key to the White House while I was there, and they never let me forget that I was in their political debt. They were not timid in demanding payment—but always for others who were in trouble, never for themselves.

In 1979, when I was president, I called for making January 15 a national holiday honoring Martin Luther King, Jr., and Coretta was by my side. And the following year, we established the Martin Luther King, Jr., National Historic Site.

When I awarded the Presidential Medal of Freedom in 1977, Coretta responded to this honor for her husband, and I quote, "This medal will be displayed with Martin's Nobel Peace Prize in the completed Martin Luther King, Jr., Center for Social Change, his official memorial in Atlanta. It will serve as a continuous reminder and inspiration to young people and unborn generations that his dream of freedom, justice, and equality must be nurtured, protected, and fully realized, that they must be keepers of the dream."

Years later in Oslo I said, "The Nobel Prize profoundly magnified the inspiring global influence of Martin Luther King, Jr., the greatest leader that my native state, and perhaps my native country, has ever produced." I was including George Washington and Abraham Lincoln and others.

On a personal note, I added, "It is unlikely that my political career beyond Georgia would have been possible without the changes brought about by the civil rights movement in the American South and throughout the nation."

This commemorative ceremony this morning and this afternoon is not only to acknowledge the great contributions of Coretta and Martin, but to remind us that the struggle for equal rights is not over. We only have to recall the color of the faces of those in Louisiana, Alabama, and Mississippi—those who were most devastated by Katrina—to know that they are not yet equal opportunities for all Americans.

It is our responsibility to continue their crusade.

I would like to say to my sister, Coretta, that we will miss you, but our sorrow is alleviated by the knowledge that you and your husband are united in glory.

Thank you for what you've meant to me and to the world.

1927 Born in Marion, Ala., into a modest family with a two-room house. As a child, Coretta picks cotton in the segregated South, but compared to other Alabama blacks her childhood is almost luxuriant: Her father works as a barber and her mother drives a school bus.

1940 Studies voice and piano at a private school. Vows to flee segregated Alabama.

1945 Graduating first in her high school class, Coretta decamps for Antioch College, Ohio, where just two years earlier her sister had been the first African-American to enroll. Majors in music and education.

1952 Hoping to become a classical singer, Coretta attends the New England Conservatory of Music, where she meets a philosophy student. "The four things that I look for in a wife are character, personality, intelligence, and beauty," Martin Luther King, Jr., says on their first date. "And you have them all." Coretta: "That's absurd. You don't even know me." (She spares him her reservations that he isn't tall enough.) A year later at their wedding ceremony, Coretta stuns Martin's father by insisting that the promise to obey be removed from the wedding vows.

1955 Rosa Parks refuses to relinquish her seat. The Montgomery Bus Boycott begins. And Martin Luther King, Jr., and his new bride stand at the center of a gathering civil rights storm. "There is a spirit and a need and a man at the beginning of every great human advance," Coretta later says. "Every one of these must be right for that particular moment of history, or nothing happens." The first of four children is born. Torn between motherhood and the movement, Coretta tells her husband, "You know I have an urge to serve just like you have." She orchestrates the first of several Freedom Concerts, combining poetry and music to raise awareness, and funds, for civil rights.

1960 The Kings move to Atlanta.

1968 Martin Luther King, Jr., is assassinated. Widowed with four children, Coretta picks up the civil rights banner even before her husband is buried—marching alongside the sanitation workers whose protest resulted in King's death hours before. Showing characteristic placidity, she claims, "I'm more determined than ever that my husband's dream will become a reality." Continuing to fight in her own fashion, she steers a course of strength and grace, focusing her laserlike attention on two goals: establishing a national holiday in King's honor and building a center to honor his memory. But she eschews reactionary anger. "Hatred is too great a burden to bear. It injures the hater more than it injures the hated."

1983 Having established the King Center, Coretta realizes her second great success. Despite conservative opposition (that includes President Reagan), Congress declares January 15 Martin Luther King, Jr., Day. But the King Center remains mired in family squabbles, never becoming the civil rights source for activism and education that Coretta envisioned. At issue: Should the center focus on King's legacy or continue his work?

1986 Travels to South Africa. Reaffirms her long-standing opposition to apartheid with a series of nonviolent protests in Washington, D.C. Later lends her support to equal rights for gays and lesbians. "Like Martin, I don't believe you can stand for freedom for one group of people and deny it to others."

2005 Suffers a serious stroke and heart attack. Misses the observance of Martin Luther King, Jr., Day for the first time in 20 years.

2006 Dies in her sleep, age 78, at a health center in Mexico. Her funeral is a six-hour affair attended by four presidents and 14,000 fans. A beloved figure to the end, she is entombed at the Martin Luther King, Jr., Center—next to her husband, reunited in a remarkable partnership that began a half century before and culminated in the tireless championship of civil rights.

JULIA CHILD

By Jacques Pépin, longtime colleague

WRITTEN IN COMMEMORATION

Julia Child was larger than life, exuberant, direct, and straight-forward. From the first time I met her in 1960 in New York, that genial, great trencherwoman swept me away with her enthusiastic self-confidence and commonsense attitude.

We often joked that we started cooking at the same time. At thirteen, I apprenticed in my hometown of Bourg-en-Bresse in 1949, and she—then in her mid-thirties—started at the Cordon Bleu in Paris the same year. Her love affair with French food would never abate. A giant of a woman with a piercing voice who had never been a chef and wasn't French, Julia became the quintessential teacher of French food techniques on television. More than anyone else, she would take the principles of French cooking and break them down in an eager American way to make them simpler and more approachable, so that people would be led into cooking.

The secret of her great success was that she made people feel comfortable. Her casual attitude, clear explanations, and willingness to try new things—even if doing so meant a mess in front of the camera . . . there was something exciting and new about her cooking, but also nourishing and heartening. It made viewers feel at ease.

Julia wanted, above all, to be a teacher of cooking. Beyond the fun, banter, and stories she relayed, there was the teaching—that was the most important thing. In a very Cartesian and practical way, she believed that cooking had rules and techniques, and she became very good at breaking down these structures to show people how to prepare her recipes.

Influential and authoritative, she was also fiercely loyal to friends, gracious to newcomers to the field, and open to other people's ideas. She was the first to admit her mistakes. She kept an open mind, whether about bioengineered food, the latest in organic food, or the newest piece of equipment on the market. But she had a clear vision of the cuisine she liked—la cuisine soignée, simple and well-prepared food—and she could meander through new food fashions without being swayed from the course she determined appropriate. She was the original antisnob, enjoying a glass of Gallo Burgundy as well as a glass of Lafite. She loved iceberg lettuce.

We had great fun cooking together in her home, in my home, on stage, on TV. We argued constantly about details: more salt, less salt; white pepper, black pepper; too thick. She was quite serious about her recipes, a stickler about details, preparing dishes over and over until they were just as she visualized them. But we always agreed on the importance of simple, clear recipes with the freshest possible ingredients, on taste above presentation, and that good food should be enjoyed with family and friends.

Her appetite for life was contagious—you knew that being with

Julia you were going to have fun. And you could rest assured that she would enjoy the food, the wine, and the company in equal measure and with great gusto. My life will almost certainly be duller now that Julia is gone. I can see her sharing a platter of oysters and a cold bottle of wine with Escoffier. And now that she has joined him, the food will be commensurably better in heaven.

1912 Born Julia Carolyn McWilliams, in Pasadena, Calif.

1934 Graduating from Smith College "with some vague idea of being a novelist or basketball star," she moves to NYC, working as a copywriter in-between cocktail parties.

1941 Turned down by the Navy for being too tall, a civic-minded Julia volunteers for the American Red Cross after the bombing of Pearl Harbor.

1946 Marries Paul Child—a high-ranking cartographer, artist and poet, 10 years older and several inches shorter.

1948 The State Department transfers the Childs to Paris. Julia recalls her first French meal of oysters, sole meuniere, and fine wine as a culinary revelation—"an opening of the soul and spirit for me." Inspired, she attends the famed Cordon Bleu and studies privately with master chefs.

1955 Teaches cooking to American women abroad, in her kitchen.

1961 Publishes her first cookbook, a 734-page tome, *Mastering the Art of French Cooking*. Making fine cuisine available to the masses, the book becomes a culinary classic—the first of her 10 best-selling cookbooks. "This is a book for the servantless American cook who can be unconcerned on occasion with budgets, waistlines, schedules, or anything else which might interfere with the enjoyment of producing something wonderful to eat."

1963 A PBS appearance leads to a regular show: *The French Chef* runs for 10 years and wins both Peabody and Emmy awards. Not always tidy in the kitchen, the 6-foot-2 folk hero in an A-line skirt preaches the delight of good food ("The only time to eat diet food is while you're waiting for the steak to cook") and concludes each show with "Bon appétit." Roasting ducks, sautéing sweetbreads, and stuffing sausages with a few well-placed grunts, she prompts the *New York Times* to write:" Child is one of the few relentlessly real people on television."

1966 Appears on the cover of *Time* as "Our Lady of the Ladle."

1978 Memorably parodied by Dan Aykroyd on *Saturday Night Live*.

1981 At the height of nutrition terror, Child eschews health food. "People are afraid of French food because of all the cream and butter. But you don't see all those big, fat people over there that you see lumbering around Disneyland."

1999 Publishes her last cookbook, *Julia and Jacques Cooking at Home* with (eulogizer) Jacques Pépin.

2001 Gives her kitchen to the Smithsonian.

2004 Dies in her home in Santa Barbara, in her sleep, at 91—having turned the art of French cooking into prime-time entertainment and elevated American food and television in the process. A towering culinary figure, she once proclaimed, "The best way to execute French cooking is to get good and loaded and whack the hell out of a chicken. Bon appétit!"

BILL W.

*By Dr. Jack Norris, close friend and
Alcoholics Anonymous trustee*

DELIVERED AT MEMORIAL SERVICE, FEBRUARY 14, 1971

ST. JOHN THE DIVINE CATHEDRAL, NEW YORK CITY

I can almost hear him saying in that half-amused, half-embarrassed way of his, "Oh come on now Jack, do you really think all this fuss is necessary?"

Two weeks ago, at a Board of Trustees meeting shortly after Bill's passing, there was a rather lively discussion about a matter involving the whole fellowship. When it had reached a certain level of intensity, I found myself waiting to hear Bill speak up, as he so often did, and say those few words that would put everything in perspective. But he didn't. And it was then that I realized way down deep that we would never hear his voice again—that we could no longer count on the constant presence of his wisdom and strength. We could never again say, as we had said so many times before, "Bill, what do you think?"

And I, at least, have not yet come to accept this completely.

Bill was no saint. He was an alcoholic and a man of stubborn will and purpose. How else could he have lived through the years of frustration, failure, and discouragement while the Steps, the Traditions, and the Conference were being hammered out on the anvil of hard experience with the first few groups? That he had the self-honesty, the clarity of vision to see the vital necessity for the Third Step, and turning one's life and will over to a Higher Power, is just one part of our great good fortune that Bill lived. I have seen Bill's pride and I have seen his humility. And I have been present when people from far countries have met him for the first time and started to cry. And all Bill—that shy Vermonter—could do was stand there and look like he wanted to run from the room. No, Bill was no saint, although many of us wanted to make him into one. Knowing this, he was insistent that legends about him be kept to a minimum; that accurate records be kept so that future generations would know him as a man. He was a very human person—to me an exceptionally human person.

Bill's constant concern was that Alcoholics Anonymous should always be available for the suffering alcoholic—that the mistakes that led to the fading of previous movements to help alcoholics should be avoided. To me, one measure of his greatness is the clarity of his vision of the future in his determination to let go of us long before we were willing to let go of him.

Bill was a good sponsor, the wise old-timer determined to relinquish the role of founder because he knew that A.A. must, as he would say, come of age and take complete responsibility for itself. He had an abiding faith that our Fellowship not only could, but should run without him. Repeatedly, during the last few years, he has said in General Service Conference sessions, "We have nothing to fear." Bill believed that the wisdom of A.A. came out of church basements and not from the pulpit; that it was directed from the groups to the Trustees rather than the other way around. He sometimes felt, though, when the Conference disagreed with him, as it sometimes did, that its conscience needed to be better informed, but it was this way that we really shared experience and developed strength and confidence that the answers would work out.

Bill knew that it was not one voice that should be heard, but many thousands of voices. And it was his gift that he was able to listen to them all, then, out of the noise and confusion, discern the group conscience. Then he would put it all together, the tension of argument would fade, and everyone would realize that his answer was right. What Bill's death means to me now is that all of us will have to listen much more carefully than we once did in order to make out the voice of the group conscience.

And I know this is possible. Bill has trained us for it, beginning in St. Louis in 1955. For this was Bill's vision: to create a channel of communication within the Fellowship of Alcoholics Anonymous that would make it possible for everyone to be here—from the individual through the group, to the delegates and to the Trustees, so that A.A. will always be here to extend a hand to the drunk who is at this very moment crying out in the darkness of his night as he reaches for help.

It has been an honor for me to have had this opportunity to participate with you in giving thanks to God that Bill lived, and was given the wisdom and strength and courage to make the world a better place for all of us. There are many more things I could say, but what can one say finally of a man's goodness and greatness? How many ways can you take his measure? I cannot do it or say it for any of you—only for myself. He was the greatest and wisest man I ever knew. Above everything, he was a man. And I believe that he left his goodness and greatness and wisdom with us, for any of us to take in what measure we can. May God grant us the wisdom and strength to keep Alcoholics Anonymous alive, vital, attractive, unencumbered by the egocentricities that can so easily spoil it.

1895 Born in small Vermont town. His father's drinking eventually destroys the family and leads to divorce.

1910 Already an inveterate perfectionist at age 15, Bill recalls, "I had to be the best at everything. Because of my perverse heart I felt myself the least of God's creatures."

1917 Age 21, prone to depression and socially awkward, Bill takes his first drink. The fiery liquid changes his life. His shyness dissolves and, he writes, "I belonged to the universe, I was a part of things at last."

1918 Marries Lois Burnham.

1929 Troubles deepen. Wilson loses his Wall Street job when the Depression hits, and begins to hibernate at home with a bottle of gin.

1934 By now, drinking has ruined his career and health. Taking his last drink, Wilson commits himself to a NYC hospital for detox—but falls into a severe depression. "It seemed as though I were at the bottom of the pit," he wrote. "I found myself crying out, 'If there is a God, let him show himself!' Suddenly, the room lit up with a great white light."

1935 Meets an alcoholic physician, Robert Smith. Their six-hour meeting convinces them of the value of one alcoholic telling his story, openly, honestly, to another. They cofound Alcoholics Anonymous. Wilson never takes another drink. One drunk helping another becomes an A.A. tradition.

1939 Publishes *Alcoholics Anonymous,* presenting the famous Twelve Steps. First step: "Admitting we are powerless over alcohol, and that our lives have become unmanageable." The Twelve Steps goes on to become a template for other recovery programs, and one of the most important spiritual/therapeutic documents ever created.

1941 NBC begins a radio program: "Is Alcohol a Problem in Your Home?"

1960 By now, Wilson is famous, but in keeping with A.A.'s commitment to anonymity is known only as Bill W. Continues to seek deeper spiritual truths. Reads voraciously. Shocks the A.A. Board by experimenting with LSD and holding séances in his home.

1969 Testifying before Congress on alcoholism, Wilson only permits photos from behind—preserving the tradition of anonymity. Refuses a *Time* magazine cover.

1971 William Griffith Wilson, 75, dies of pneumonia in Miami. Thousands learn for the first time the name of the man who helped them recover from alcoholism. A Washington A.A. member says, "From Harold Hughes to the man on the Bowery, there's not a person in A.A. who doesn't know that if it weren't for Bill W., we'd all be dead." Survived by his wife Lois, who helped him start Al-Anon for families of alcoholics, Bill W. summed up his philosophy: "Don't drink. One day at a time. Go to meetings." Today, A.A. boasts 2.2 million members in over 150 countries around the world.

ALFRED KINSEY

By Helen D'Amico, secretary and friend

WRITTEN IN COMMEMORATION

I first met Dr. Kinsey in the fall, 1937. I was an entering fresh-man at Indiana, and he hired me to join his staff of four girls who "mounted bugs" in his etymology lab. At eighteen any full professor was an awesome sight, and since this man who had writ-ten numerous textbooks and scientific articles was to be my em-ployer, I placed him on a higher pedestal than the others.

Once he had hired me I was one of his "family"—and he was the unquestioned patriarch. All of us who worked for him were a little frightened of him, though we had no reason to be. Beneath his briskness he was kind and considerate. The minute it was possible he went to great trouble to secure raises from thirty to thirty-five cents an hour for each of us. We had keys to the office, and he al-lowed us to work whenever it was convenient for us, and for as many hours a month as we could arrange. He invited us to musicales at his home and to enjoy his beautiful garden. We respected this man.

He realized the need for physical exercise and outside interests: For exercise he worked in his garden, a showplace. He was not willing to "putter" with his plants; he strenuously and scientifically applied himself to this activity. The same with his love for music. When he listened to a good record or went to a concert, he lost himself in the music—the life of the composer, orchestra history, strain of a single violin, all were neatly cataloged bits of knowledge to be enjoyed, analyzed, shared with friends.

His work, his play, his recreation—in each he sought perfection, and at each he overworked, overextended himself. He had great self-discipline. In every detail, he was precise in his work and expected the same from those who worked for him. On the surface, his great thirst for knowledge created a rather austere figure, but underneath he was understanding and tolerant of human foibles.

After college I left Bloomington. I wrote to Dr. Kinsey occasionally telling him of my progress. Busy as he was, he always answered with a short note assuring he was glad to hear from me.

Quite by chance, I became his secretary in 1947. During the years I had traveled extensively and had some interesting jobs abroad. When I stopped to visit him that summer, I was no longer frightened of him. We had a pleasant visit, but I was amazed when the next day this man who was so thorough and exact in everything offered me an important position on his staff. I assured him that my stenography was poor, and felt he should get someone more qualified for the position. My salary demands were beyond his budget. I had definite plans to return abroad. But he persisted, and if he wanted something he got it. At the time I thought he was being rather naïve and hurried in hiring me, but later I understood. I had been a member of his "family" and one of his flock had returned to the fold. Dr. Kinsey was a devout family man.

During the two years I was his secretary I came to know him well, and liked what I knew. The original work he did at the institute, such a controversial subject, no one else could have done. He realized the delicate nature of the endeavor and didn't allow any other staff member to do anything independently—though he was most liberal in publicly acclaiming their contributions. Even the most mundane of the routine tasks at the office were checked and rechecked by him. He was so absorbed in his work that he secured hired help for his garden, lost his close touch with music, and even gave up his work on the gall wasps, finally even selling his huge collection of insects. Dr. Kinsey relaxed when he was working. Eight hours a day wasn't enough—he found peace in doing eight hours extra.

To those who did not know him well, Dr. Kinsey seemed a formidable man. This was only his appearance. In his unique way he was one of the most considerate men I have ever known. He was devoted to his staff and, I am sure, felt a real affection for each of us.

A word about Mrs. Kinsey. During the height of Dr. Kinsey's publicity, the joke "Is there a Mrs. Kinsey?" crossed the nation. Clara Kinsey made it possible for her husband to be the great man he was and accomplish the things he did. She was his silent partner, and the one person who truly knew and understood him. Theirs was a great love. Mrs. Kinsey —"Mac"—is an intelligent woman who chose to make a career of her husband and family, and she remained a quiet rock of strength waiting in the background.

Dr. Kinsey's death can be attributed to "overwork." But his life would have ended years earlier if he had not overworked, overproduced. This was his life.

1894 Born in tenement town of Hoboken, N.J., to conservative parents. An autocrat and ardent prohibitionist, his father takes the family to church on every possible occasion: three times on Sunday, plus assorted mid-week services.

....

1902 A delicate and unhealthy child, Alfred contracts a variety of uncommon diseases: typhoid fever, rheumatic fever, and rickets—which will keep Kinsey from the draft.

....

1912 Graduates high school as class valedictorian.

....

1916 Graduating from Bowdoin College, Kinsey heads for Harvard. Teaching zoology while pursuing his doctorate, he comes to believe that science holds the key—truth—with which humanity can uplift itself.

....

1920 Hired by Indiana University as specialist on plant and insect life. Salary: $2,000/year. Becomes leading authority on the gall wasp.

....

1921 Marries Clara McMillen. Although their wedding night doesn't go as planned—they try for a year before consummating their marriage—they go on to have four children, and an open relationship.

....

1938 Kinsey's interest in sex is sparked: Asked to teach a sex education course preparing students for fulfilling marriages, he is shocked by rampant misconceptions. His open support of contraception leads the I.U. administration to quickly replace him—further stoking the fires of his curiosity.

....

1942 Rockefeller Foundation funds Kinsey's research, and he begins his famous study of sexuality, going on to employ 14 researchers, who interview 18,000 bootleggers, clergymen, clerks, clinical psychologists, housewives, lawyers, marriage counselors, ne'er-do-wells, and persons in the social register. Each interviewer asks up to 500 extremely personal questions. Six years later, the resulting *Sexual Behavior in the Human Male* appears in an explosion of publicity. Astonishing conclusions: (1) One in ten men is homosexual; (2) 90% of males masturbate; and

(3) 85% had premarital intercourse. Kinsey: "The only unnatural sex act is that which you cannot perform."

1947 Founds Institute for Sex Research.

1948 Despite hefty $6.50 price and scientific tone, *Sexual Behavior in the Human Male* sells 500,000 copies—catapulting Kinsey from obscure wasp expert to best-selling sexologist. Newspapers, magazines, and women's clubs discuss at length.

1952 Under pressure, Rockefeller Foundation discontinues $100,000/year grant.

1953 Publishes sequel, *Sexual Behavior in the Human Female*—but due to widely published excerpts and Communist hysteria, it suffers an icy reception. Kinsey appears on cover of *Time*. The Reece committee, a red-chasing arm of Congress, accuses Kinsey of destroying American morals and making the country vulnerable to takeover—through sex.

1956 Depressed, midway through research on sex in prison, the father of sexology dies of a heart attack, age 62, Clara at his side. Having championed sexual freedom—and the belief that sex was both good and necessary—Kinsey set the stage for the sexual revolution of the sixties and the pursuit of sex for its own sake. Mae West: "If Kinsey is right, I do what comes naturally."

KAREN SILKWOOD

By Michael Meadows, son

DELIVERED AT 25TH ANNIVERSARY MEMORIAL SERVICE,
DECEMBER 17, 1999
SYMPHONY SPACE, NEW YORK CITY

Marianne Williamson once suggested that our deepest fear is not that we are inadequate. Our deepest fear is that we are powerful beyond measure. It is our light, not our darkness, which most frightens us.

Twenty-five years ago a young woman whose beliefs would not allow her to be silent was killed on a lonely highway just north of Oklahoma City. She was killed because she believed that she was morally obligated to protect the rights of her fellow man, to stand up against corporate oppression and shout aloud for those who were afraid to speak for themselves. She did this without promise of fame or reward. She did it not knowing that she would go down in history. She did it quite simply because she knew it was the right thing to do.

Many times in my life I have had to make some tough decisions. It isn't always easy to choose the right way, and there have been times in my life when I haven't. Times when I took the path of least resistance. But there have also been times in my life when, faced with tough choices, I opened my eyes and my heart as well and asked, "Lord, what should I do?"

I believe that it is at those times in my life that He lets me hear the voice of that heroic young woman. That headstrong, self-confident, ever-determined voice. She might say to me, "Michael, you listen to what your heart says, you make up your mind to do something and you will do the right thing. I have faith in you, son."

I'll never get to hear those words from her mouth myself. The young woman died when I was a very small child. I often wonder what it would have been like to meet her, to know her not as a five-year-old boy, but as the man I have become. I would like to have had at least one adult conversation with the woman who made such an impact, not just on the lives of myself and my sisters, but on the lives of countless other people around the world.

Sometimes I wake up in the early morning from a dream and think that I can see her there in the room with me. I think that she stays around for those first few seconds after waking to let me know that she is watching me. And that she is waiting for me to let my own light shine.

I love you, Mother.

1946 Born in Longview, Tex., to William and Merle Silkwood.

1963 Attending Nederland High School, Karen is a member of the school band, science club, and the National Honor Society. Her yearbook quote: "It is not only the most difficult thing in the world to know one-self, but the most inconvenient thing, too."

1964 Studies medical technology at Lamar State College, on a scholarship from the Business and Professional Women's Club.

1965 Marries William Meadows. Three children follow.

1972 Losing custody of her children in divorce, Silkwood decamps for Oklahama City, where she is hired by Kerr McGee, a plutonium plant. Initially delighted with her $4/hour job, Silkwood notices poor health and safety practices and becomes active in the Oil, Chemical, and Atomic Workers Union. Because Kerr McGee is a "respectable" company supported by the Atomic Energy Commission, and unemployment is rampant, she has trouble marshalling support.

1973 Begins gathering evidence of unsafe conditions. Despite union warnings to work quietly, Silkwood is increasingly vocal. Her phone is bugged, her movement monitored, and, in the first of several unexplained contaminations, she suffers plutonium exposure.

1974 Armed with evidence of unsafe conditions, leaks, and missing plutonium, Silkwood decides to go public with her findings. En route to meet a *New York Times* reporter, she is killed in an auto crash. The evidence is never found. An autopsy shows rampant plutonium contamination—so severe that her belongings are placed in steel drums to avoid secondary contamination. Dead at 28, Silkwood is buried in a Texas cemetery. Her death leads to a federal investigation into plant safety, and ushers in a new era of corporate accountability.

1975 Kerr McGee closes the plant and—still refusing to admit liability—pays Silkwood's family $1.38 million.

1983 Meryl Streep brings *Silkwood* to the screen—immortalizing the nuclear martyr who destroyed nuclear energy's image as a clean and safe power source.

SIGMUND FREUD

By Stefan Zweig, close friend

DELIVERED AT FUNERAL, SEPTEMBER 16, 1939
LONDON CREMATORY, ENGLAND

With other mortals, their lives come to an end the moment their bodies expire. His departure is not an end—a harsh close to a life—but an unwitting transition from mortality to immortality.

Don't expect me to praise Sigmund Freud's life's work here. You are all privy to his achievements. Is there anyone among us who is not? Who has not been shaped and changed deeply by his thoughts? His magnificent discovery of the human psyche is alive in all languages. Where is there a language without the concepts and vocabulary wrested from the twilight of the semiconscious? Like no other contemporary, he has enriched and reevaluated ethics, education, philosophy, poetry, and psychology, alongside all forms of spiritual and artistic creation. All are indebted to him. Every one of us twentieth-century denizens would be different minus his thoughts and insights; think, judge, and feel more narrowly, less freely, without his ability to anticipate our thoughts, without that powerful inward thrust that he has bestowed on us.

Only the mortal Sigmund Freud has left us, precious and irreplaceable friend.

In our youth we desired nothing more fervently than to lead a heroic life. We entertained dreams of meeting such a spiritual hero in the flesh, a hero who would help us better ourselves, a man who was oblivious to the temptations of fame and vanity, who possessed a complete and responsible soul, dedicated to his mission, a mission that reaps not its own benefits but enriches all of mankind. Our dear departed Freud fulfilled this enthusiastic dream of our youth. There he was in vain and unforgettable times, single-mindedly driven by his search for the truth—he who valued nothing in the world but the absolute. There he was, the most noble of researchers with unrelenting doubt. He would carefully examine all aspects of a problem, reflecting on it, doubting himself for as long as he was not entirely certain of an insight, and then, once he had wrestled with an idea until the very end, he defended it against the objections and resistance of the entire world.

His example taught us, once again, there is no greater courage on earth than the one exemplified by the free, independent spiritual human being. He was willing to embrace any risk despite all objections and criticisms; he ventured on untraveled ground until the very last day of his life.

Yet, we who knew him personally, also remember the touching modesty that resided alongside his courage—he was understanding of weakness in the souls of others. At the end of his life, this profound duality between the rigorous mind and the gentle heart led to a complete harmony in the realm of spirit: a pure and clarified, autumnal wisdom. Those who witnessed his final years found consolation during an hour of intimate conversation with him about the absurdity and madness of our times. During such hours, I often wished they could be shared with younger people so that, when they will no longer be able to bear witness to the spiritual greatness of this man, they would be able to assert proudly: I have been in the presence of a truly wise man, I have known Sigmund Freud.

At this hour of death, we are comforted by the knowledge that he finished his work and completed the formation of his innermost self. Through his courage of spirit and patience of his soul he was able to lord over life and physical pain. His battle against suffering was no less fierce than his battle against the personification of the supposedly incomprehensible: he was an exemplary physician as well as a philosopher, adhering until the last bitter moment to the Socratic dictum "Know thyself."

Thank you for the example you gave us, dear and revered friend. Thank you for your deeds and accomplishments. Thank you for all that you have represented and for what you implanted in our souls. Thank you for the worlds that you have opened for us but which we must now travel alone without your guidance—forever faithful to you, in awe of you, our precious friend, Sigmund Freud.

1856 Born in Morovia—a Hungarian province. Attending Sigmund's birth, a peasant woman predicts his greatness.

1873 Perpetually at the top of his class, Freud enters the University of Vienna. Nonreligious by upbringing, he graduates an even stronger atheist, convinced of the strictly scientific nature of the world.

1885 Studying psychiatry, Freud develops new theories on neurotic disorders—making a lifelong enemy out of his orthodox mentor and launching a pattern of revolution. His own students, including Jung and Adler, will later diverge from Freud in much the same way.

1886 Marries Martha Bernays. Six children follow.

1887 Introduces hypnotic suggestion, claiming, "The mind is an iceberg—it floats with only one-seventh of its bulk above water."

1900 Publishes *The Interpretation of Dreams*.

1902 Returns to Vienna to become professor of neurology. Using his apartment as a clinic, Freud continues developing theories—offering a wealth of remarkable ideas amidst a quickly growing conservatism. His work on hysteria becomes widely known, postulating that hysteria is the result of a shock—probably sexual in nature—and that attendant memories have been repressed. Psychoanalysis is a way to recall the memory and remove the hysteria.

1906 Befriends Carl Jung. They travel in the U.S., giving lectures on psychoanalysis. Freud's analysis: "America is a country of unthinking optimism and a shallow philosophy."

1923 Publishes *The Ego and the Id.*

1930 Freud receives the greatest cultural distinction in Germany: the Goethe Prize—but he is ravaged with cancer and cannot attend. By now, Freudian terms such as *repression, transference,* and *neurosis* have entered pop culture.

1936 On his 80th birthday, Freud is toasted by even his bitterest critics. Although his works are the subject of great alienation, he is described by friends as a gentle and considerate man "when not talking shop."

1937 "It is tragic when a man outlives his body," he says of his debilitating cancer. Although the annexation of Austria by Germany appears likely,

Freud refuses to leave, telling friends he would kill himself if the Nazis took his library. The following year when his books are burned in a bonfire that consumes non-Aryan works, Freud remarks, "At least I have been burned in good company."

1939 Dies shortly before midnight, age 83, at his son's home in Hampstead, England—having bequeathed a deeper understanding of the psyche, a clutch of psychological terms, and a new respect for the mine-strewn years of youth.

MAHATMA GANDHI

By Jawaharlal Nehru, prime minister and close friend

DELIVERED AT MEMORIAL SERVICE, FEBRUARY 2, 1948
NEW DELHI, INDIA

A glory has departed and the sun that warmed and brightened our lives has set, and we shiver in the cold and dark. Yet he would not have us feel this way. After all, that man with divine fire changed us—we have been molded by him during these years. And so if we praise him, we also praise ourselves. Great men have monuments in bronze and marble set up for them, but this man of divine fire managed in his lifetime to become enshrined in millions and millions of hearts, so that all of us became the stuff that he was made of—though to an infinitely lesser degree. He spread out in this way all over India. Not just in palaces, or in select places or in assemblies, but in every hamlet and hut of the lowly and those who suffer.

What, then, can we say about him except to feel humble on this occasion? It is almost doing him an injustice just to pass him by with words, when he demanded work and labor and sacrifice from us. In a large measure he made this country, during the last thirty years or more, attain unequaled heights of sacrifice. He succeeded in that. And he suffered tremendously, though his tender face never lost its smile and he never spoke a harsh word to anyone. But he suffered—suffered for the failing of this generation whom he had trained, suffered because we went away from the path that he had shown us. And ultimately the hand of a child of his—for his killer is as much a child of his as any other Indian—the hand of a child of his struck him down.

History will judge this period that we have passed through. It will judge the successes and the failures—we are too near it to be proper judges and to understand what has happened, and what has not. All we know is that there was a glory and that it is no more. All we know is that for the moment there is darkness, not so dark certainly, because when we look into our hearts we still find the living flame which he lighted there. And if those living flames exist, there will not be darkness in this land, and we shall be able, remembering him and following his path, to illumine this land again, small as we are, but with the fire that he instilled.

He was the greatest symbol of the India of the past—and of the India of the future—that we could have had. We stand on this edge of the present, between that past and the future, and we face all manner of perils. The greatest peril is the lack of faith, the sense of frustration that comes to us, the sinking of the heart and of the spirit when we see ideals go overboard, when we see the great things we talked about pass into empty words, and life taking a different course. Yet, this period will pass soon enough.

He has gone, and all over India there is a feeling of desolation. All of us sense that feeling, and I do not know how to get rid of it.

Yet with that feeling there is also a feeling of proud thankfulness for this mighty person. In ages to come, centuries and maybe millennia after us, people will think of this generation when this man of God trod on earth, and will think of us who, however small, could also follow his path and tread the holy ground where his feet had been.

Let us be worthy of him.

1869 Born Mohandas Gandhi, in Podbandar, into the trading caste.

1872 Age 13, marries Kasturba Nakanji, age 10.

1888 Over the objection of elders, the 19-year-old Gandhi sets sail for England to study law—promising his mother to abstain from wine, women, and meat.

1893 Career languishing, Gandhi sails for Johannesburg where he encounters his first taste of European racism: "Coolies" and nonwhites aren't permitted in first-class railway cars. Refusing to leave, Gandhi is summarily escorted off the train, his luggage tossed onto the platform.

1904 Publishes *The Indian Option*, the first of his many newspapers.

1915 After 20 years of practicing law in South Africa, returns to India, where he travels widely and conducts a fast on behalf of Asian immigrants— laying the groundwork for future nonviolent protests.

1919 Launches Civil Disobedience campaign: Indians must withdraw from British institutions and learn the art of self-reliance. Arrested for sedition, Gandhi is sentenced to six years in prison and anointed with the title *Mahatma*, "Great Soul."

1930 With his Civil Disobedience campaign in full swing, at age 61, Gandhi leads a 165-mile march to the Arabian Sea where, in defiance of British monopoly on salt production, he evaporates sea water to produce the commodity, breaking the law. Arrested again.

1932 Begins a "fast unto death" to protest British treatment of Untouchables—whom Gandhi calls "God's children." After 6 days of fasting, he secures a pact improving their status.

1942 Calls for independence from British rule, giving Indians the mantra "Do or Die," and asking them to lay down their lives for freedom.

1947 England surrenders India—a major victory for Gandhi and the principles of nonviolence. In search of common ground between Hindus and Muslims, Gandhi walks from village to village, nursing the wounded and consoling the widowed. Even his detractors concede these are his finest years. "You must not lose faith in humanity. Humanity is an ocean; if a few drops of the ocean are dirty, the ocean does not become dirty."

1948 At the end of a five-day fast, Gandhi is shot by a Hindi extremist while en route to evening prayers. Falling to the ground, he blesses his assassin. His timepiece stops at the minute of his death: 5:12 P.M. In Hindu fashion, his body is carried on a wooden cot covered with a white sheet to a funeral pyre, where it is burned—the ashes scattered on the holy Jumna River.

ALBERT SCHWEITZER

By Walter Munz, disciple and close friend

DELIVERED AT MEMORIAL EVENING, OCTOBER 13, 2000

WORLD PEACE SYMPOSIUM, NASHVILLE, TENNESSEE

E ven when I was a boy, he made a deep impression on me. My first contact with him was in his books, where I found him a formidable thinker and theologian, a connoisseur of Bach, and a doctor deeply familiar with Africa. As Albert Schweitzer lived what he so vividly described, it became clear to me that this man was a great figure.

In 1961, as a young doctor, I was fortunate enough to be able to go to Lambarene. I spent over ten working years in Africa and for the last four and a half years of his life, I met with Albert Schweitzer almost every day. When he died, it fell on me to make the speech of farewell and thanks—surrounded by a veritable throng of grief-stricken black and white people, Albert's daughter Rena, and the nurses, doctors, and other hospital staff. We were all moved and deter-mined that the work in this hospital should be continued in his spirit.

I owe much to Albert Schweitzer and his Lambarene. The men, women, and children of Africa left their mark on me: I met my wife in Lambarene, where she worked as the hospital midwife for seven years. We returned to Lambarene in 1980. Our family song is in two-part harmony: one voice sings a European melody, but the other is accompanied by the joyful and mournful sounds of Africa.

Today, I present to you Albert Schweitzer the doctor, the thinker, the artist, and the man deeply devoted to God. He was all of these things at the same time, which is why he radiated goodness. The man of medicine and the man of ethics were a completely insepa-rable whole.

The first time he returned from Lambarene, he wrote the following:

"What has the white man of all nations done to the black peo-ple since these distant lands were discovered? What does it mean to us that so many peoples have died out after being visited by Euro-peans calling themselves Christians? A burden of guilt rests on us and on our civilization. We are not free to choose whether or not we do good to those people—it is simply something we have to do. The good we do is not charity but atonement."

Can you hear the revolutionary thinking in these ideas? The year was 1920. Such words were alien to the spirit of the times.

I could talk forever about Schweitzer's work as a doctor: about the clarity and attention to detail of his handwritten operation re-ports and drawings, about his endeavors for the spiritual and med-ical welfare of his patients, about the practicality with which he built his hospital village and ran it with an order that did justice to the people and to Africa. An intelligent man in Lambarene wrote: "Albert Schweitzer had the knack of interfering as little as possible with our African ways." But the most important word about Schweitzer is the African word *Nkengo*—"mercifulness." *Nkengo,* that was the word that I heard most frequently when natives spoke about their Grand Docteur.

The memory of Albert Schweitzer still lives on in every village in the country. In many an African heart the doctor has been kept in a sort of loving memorial.

In 1964 in Lambarene, he summed up his thought on the reverence for life:

"I appeal to mankind to adopt the ethics of reverence for life. These ethics make no distinction between valuable and less valuable, superior and lower life. They reject such a distinction. For who of us knows what significance the other creature has intrinsically and in the world as a whole? The fact uppermost in the mind of man is: 'I am life that wants to live, in the midst of life that wants to live.' The man who has thus become a thinker feels the necessity to regard any will to live with the same reverence to life as he does to his own."

To see how Schweitzer lived his reverence for life, look at any given day. Two examples:

In Lambarene, it was taken for granted that every nurse, doctor, and staff member had their own domestic pet. Mr. Schweitzer had the Alsatian Porto, the dachshund Tschutschu, and the parrot Kudeku. For over two years I had a female chimp, Branca. You can imagine the thousand ways we became attached to these animals. Our community with them was not consciously thought out—it happened of its own accord. It was the manifestation of a sort of Franciscan community with all creatures. We also had a bad-tempered turkey with a fondness for pecking at the calves of nurses. The Grand Docteur used to defend this feathered creature by saying, "The turkey is also one of us. He and I have something in common: we both imagine we are the boss in this hospital, so we just have to put up with him."

Another example: The hospital had 620 beds for sick people,

twenty pens for sick dogs, sheep, goats, antelopes, apes, and pelicans. But Schweitzer also treated plants. When I asked about this, the cook Massandi Josef showed me a large mango tree with two trunks. One trunk bore a huge crown, the other ended somewhat abruptly and was topped with a cement cap. Massandi told me that some years earlier the tree had been struck by lightning and one of the trunks had been broken. The doctor had bound up the wound—first by sprinkling earth on the wood, then pouring cement over it and pressing down firmly with his hands. Massandi continued, "You see, the great doctor wants to help God protect all the things he made."

And Schweitzer the artist? I watched and listened to Mr. Schweitzer make music when he was ninety. He went to the piano about an hour before dinner. In the twilight, and later in the warm glow of the oil lamp which stood on the piano, he played—without music. His hands were broad, sinewy, veined, sunburnt, almost like those of a gardener or farmer. At any rate, hands that were used to hard work.

He started off with scales, trills, increasingly complicated runs and flourishes, then went on to produce sounds quite slowly, followed by a series of chords—and back to scales again. It was as if the old man was preparing for another concert tour. He played the notes with great precision and joined them together like a master builder. If a melody didn't quite work, he played it over and over, speeding up the tempo until he had mastered the passage and could play it slowly and confidently. What surprised me about Schweitzer—not just in music—was the bewildering combination of activities: writing letters, discussions, pushing wheelbarrows, feeding hens, holding a service, making music . . . one after the other. All in its own good time and as peacefully as you please.

Schweitzer's reverence for life didn't just have philosophical roots. It burst forth from the depths of his piety. When the Africans asked him why he had come to them he replied, "The Lord Jesus asked me to come to the Ogowe River." That the Grand Docteur held a service in his hospital every Sunday was at the very heart of his work in Africa. And every evening after dinner, until about six days before he died, he held a service with singing, Bible reading, and prayers.

So what will the future hold? What do we say to our children and grandchildren? It is important to bear testimony to what Albert Schweitzer achieved. We should not expect the world to be improved by organizations, party programmes, and structural changes—but by our own thinking. Each of us should accept responsibility for some undertaking and seek our own response to Jesus's commandment "Rise up and follow me!"—just as Albert Schweitzer sought and found his own response.

I would like to leave you with three of his phrases:

"The peace of God is not rest but driving force."

"There is not just one Lambarene, everyone can have his Lambarene."

"I believe in the future of this age, but it is up to us to shape it."

1875 Born in Germany, in the storybook village of Haute Alsace.

1883 Showing potential as musical prodigy, he begins playing church organ, even though his feet barely touch the pedals.

1893 Enters University of Strasbourg as philosophy student.

1905 Over vigorous protests from his friends, Schweitzer decides to become a physician in equatorial Africa, explaining, "I want to be a doctor and work without having to talk. For years, I have been giving myself out in words." Studies medicine for next seven years.

1912 Not yet through with words, Schweitzer publishes *Paul and His Inter-preters*—a religious treatise on rebirth. Marries Helene Bresslau, daughter of a well-known historian.

1913 Schweitzer sails for Africa, where he builds Lamberene—a medical and missionary station scratched out of the jungle. The facility grows to 70 buildings, 350 beds, and a leper village of 200. But sticklers for sterilization are aghast: Patients are encouraged to bring family members to cook, leper babies crawl in unpaved streets, and animals wander in and out—including a hippo fond of the vegetable garden. Schweitzer: "Simple people need simple healing methods."

1914 WWI breaks out. Schweitzer and wife are prisoners of war.

1915 Traveling through a herd of hippos, Schweitzer is struck by the phrase "reverence for life"—leading to an enduring ethical system for the medical community. Reverence has repercussions at Lamberene: Mosquitoes are not swatted. Bugs are not doused with chemicals. And building is often brought to a halt, lest ant nests be harmed.

1919 Daughter Rhena is born.

1923 Publishes *The Philosophy of Civilization*, a review of ethical thought—also his masterwork.

1949 Visits the U.S. Musician, theologian, scholar, doctor, lecturer, missionary, writer, builder, and humanitarian—Schweitzer is a modern Renaissance man, bringing rationality to religion. Thousands flock to his lectures. A tall, extremely handsome man, Schweitzer has mellowed into a softer, aged version of himself—gray-haired and less severe, but still determined to revere life.

1952 Receives Nobel Peace Prize—the latest tribute in a collection of medals, degrees, special stamps, and scrolls.

1957 After working at Schweitzer's side, Helene dies. Schweitzer commits his remaining days to Lamberene.

1965 Celebrates his 90th birthday amidst hundreds of well-wishing Africans. Months later, he dies in his own jungle hospital, from circulatory trouble brought on by old age. Buried on the banks of the Ogooue River, Schweitzer's grave is marked by a cross he made himself. Hospital workers, cripples, lepers, and other patients gather in the jungle heat as the body of the noted doctor, philosopher, scholar, and musician is lowered into the ground. The hospital is handed over to his assistant (and eulogizer) Walter Munz.

ELISABETH KÜBLER-ROSS

By David Kessler, coauthor and friend

DELIVERED AT MEMORIAL SERVICE, SEPTEMBER 4, 2004
SCOTTSDALE BIBLE CHURCH, SCOTTSDALE, ARIZONA

For being the legendary expert on death and dying, she was the most alive person I have ever met.

She loved food, but she was never hungry. She would, on occasion, be starving. She had a refined palate. I once asked her, on my way from the airport, if she needed anything, and she said, "I need some bread. Please bring some bread, I am starving for some bread." I grabbed the first loaf of bread I found, rushed in with the bread like I was saving her life. She took one look at the pre-sliced white loaf and threw it across the room. "This is not bread. Go look in my kitchen and you will see real bread."

She had a voracious appetite for bread and for life. If I did something stupid, I was sure to get a karate chop. You weren't really in the game until you had gotten a karate chop from Elisabeth. Like doing something really offensive such as offering her a piece of her fine Swiss chocolate but referring to it as candy. A mortal sin.

She liked to be called Elisabeth. She would get mad at me if I ever, even in a documentary, referred to her as Elisabeth Kübler-Ross. She was just Elisabeth; she was not a formal person at all.

Years ago, I was going on a trip to Egypt that featured notable speakers on death and dying. I was a minor speaker and Elisabeth was the main attraction.

Unfortunately, that was when she had her first stroke and couldn't make the trip. When I returned, I called her son Ken to see how she was doing and he said, "Why don't you call her directly?"

I did, expressing my disappointment that we didn't have the opportunity to really get to know one another. I said I hoped someday our paths would cross again. Elisabeth said, "How about Tuesday?"

So began our nine-year friendship and relationship as writing partners.

[He looks over the podium at Elisabeth.] This is actually very unnerving. This is the quietest she has ever been in my presence.

Elisabeth told me on our first meeting that she smelled people to see who is real and who is a phony baloney. She thought I smelled good—since I was still smoking at the time, I smelled like cigarettes. Little did I know that that was her favorite fragrance.

Elisabeth's health was fragile. She always said, when you are with the ill, ask them what they need. So I asked, "Elisabeth, what do you need?" Some people say, I need to cry, or some need to talk; others need to be held. Elisabeth said, "I need my air-conditioning filter changed right away."

Elisabeth was very real. Many people here will understand that she had a kind of honesty that you would either admire or it would make you extremely mad at her. That same honesty that offended many also made her stand out. She cared about no one else's opinion. But she cared about people that no one else cared for.

She was enormously passionate about any injustice in the world, didn't matter what, didn't matter who. She distained injustice.

Working with Elisabeth on our first book, *Life Lessons,* was not like other professional experiences I'd had. It was much more personal, challenging and always adventurous. I learned early on that one day at a time was not enough for our work—since it always began with lunch and then shopping, then tea, and then shopping over the phone from some catalog. I could never have imagined, in as hot a climate as Phoenix, that the Burlington Coat Factory would be so important to her. She *loved* the Burlington Coat Factory. (Thank God she had a daughter that lived in a cold climate.)

After the meals and shopping on our "second day of work," I was so desperate to finish the writing that we had started on the prior day, I resorted to taking her cigarettes away.

It was a tricky thing to do, but playing it safe with Elisabeth was the most dangerous thing one could do. She would get one cigarette an hour. I thought it might be the end of our writing together, but Elisabeth understood delayed gratification; and, on subsequent visits she would jokingly surrender her cigarettes or lighter. She said she couldn't help herself, she loved to be bad.

I have a ton of memories of hundreds of hours together.

One day while discussing favorite movies we found we shared a common love for *Oh, God.* She loved the idea of a comedian like George Burns as God. Elisabeth loved to laugh. And when it came to religion, she never felt compelled to join one. She loved the spirituality of all. Over a week at her house, you could meet a rabbi, a priest, a nun, a Buddhist monk, a channeler, shaman, and healer. You get the picture.

She loved to talk about her kids; she was so proud they were their own people. But it wasn't just her kids or her rules she loved—and loved to break rules. She loved to be bad. Two years ago, when she was hospitalized and we thought she was dying, she was disappointed that I had followed the rule of "No visitors under the age of fourteen" in the hospital, and that I had my kids waiting in the hospital lobby. "Haven't I taught you anything about working with the dying?" she said. "Sneak them up immediately."

Even this summer, I thought Elisabeth could no longer smoke. But suddenly she said, last month, "Let's go outside." On the way out, she said, "Third drawer cigarettes; lighter behind the books." Outside she lit up, and I held an ashtray for her. She purposely missed the astray. I said, "Elisabeth you did that on purpose."

"You are so in the box, and I bet you draw inside the lines," she replied.

She loved to work. People would bring over students and she would teach. People would come in grief and she would counsel, and when we turned in our last book barely a month ago, she said, I am done. And I thought, yeah until the next project. But Elisabeth's first book was *On Death and Dying,* and it is fitting that we just finished *On Grief and Grieving.* This time she really was done.

She had a strong heart, and a kind one. At eight years old, she cared about the girl in the next hospital bed more than she worried about her health. Whether it was a friend in childhood, a baby with AIDS, or even her bunny, her heart was immense. Look at how many people are here today. Imagine how many of us are carrying on her work. And in her last hours of life, the end seemed long. That same big heart did not want to stop beating.

I am sorry to be schmaltzy, Elisabeth, but, Good job! Good life! Congratulations on your graduation. As she said, it is not for us to say that she has died, but to say, "God did she live."

A memorial service is a celebration of life, and that's what she wanted. And that this person mattered so much and contributed greatly—this is also a real loss. I miss her and I am sad to be without her. And everyone here probably represents a thousand who could not be here and who all were touched by her life. Although I want to both celebrate her life and honor the loss, I don't want to get glib in the celebration nor get lost in the loss, but find a place where I hold both. I will miss her beyond words and I am happy for her; and so relieved that she is no longer confined to a body, or confined to a bed or confined to even this world. Elisabeth was always too big to be contained.

1926 Born in Zurich, Switzerland—the first of triplets, weighing scarcely two pounds.

1934 A schoolmate dies of meningitis. Elisabeth is moved by her farm village, which gathers around to memorialize the dead child. "There was a feeling of solidarity, of common tragedy shared."

1939 In sixth grade, declares her intention to become a physician.

1943 Volunteers at Zurich hospital, helping refugees from Nazi Germany. When WWII ends, she hitchhikes through nine war-torn countries— opening first-aid posts and working on reconstruction projects along the way. Develops skills as mason, roofer, and cook. Visiting a concentration camp, her life comes into focus, and she decides to become psychiatrist helping people cope with death.

1957 Enrolls in University of Zurich medical school. Marries American doctor Emmanuel K. Ross the following year.

1960 As research fellow at Manhattan State hospital, Kübler-Ross is appalled by treatment of dying patients. "They were shunned and abused—sometimes kept in hot tubs with water up to their necks for up to 24 hours." After much pestering, Ross is allowed to develop individual care programs.

A Wonderful Life

1962 Begins teaching at University of Colorado School of Medicine. Her classes draw standing-room-only audiences—especially after she wheels in a 16-year-old patient dying of leukemia, who moves the class to tears. "Now you're acting like human beings instead of scientists," Kübler-Ross tells them.

1969 Publishes best seller *On Death and Dying*, postulating five stages of death: (1) denial, (2) anger, (3) bargaining, (4) depression, (5) acceptance. Based on thousands of interviews with patients and health-care workers, the book ends the centuries-old taboo of openly discussing death. "Those who have the strength and the love to sit with a dying patient in the silence that goes beyond words will know that this moment is neither frightening nor painful, but a peaceful cessation of the functioning of the body."

1985 Thanks to Kübler-Ross, health-care education now addresses the subject. *On Death and Dying* becomes an indispensable manual. Hospices begin to flourish.

1987 Publishes *The Wheel of Life: A Memoir of Living and Dying*, postulating that "death can be one of the greatest experiences ever. If you live each day of your life right, then you have nothing to fear.'"

1990 Begins focusing her energies on the afterlife—claiming proof, culled from thousands of near-death interviews, that the hereafter is more serene. Scientists balk. When several of her centers are burned to the ground, she moves to Arizona in 1994 to be near her son Ken.

2004 After revolutionizing the care of dying, and enabling millions to die with greater dignity, Ross succumbs to the great mystery she wrote about— at 78, in her home in Scottsdale, Arizona, claiming, "I'm going to dance in all the galaxies."

MEDIA TITANS

EDWARD R. MURROW

By Charles Kuralt, coworker and admirer

DELIVERED AT MEMORIAL EVENING, APRIL 1971
NORTH CAROLINA LITERARY AND HISTORICAL ASSOCIATION

I speak here of a man who, it seemed to me at the time I knew him, was the best man I have ever known. Nothing has happened since then to make me alter that judgment. Others who knew him far better than I shared that feeling. He was not the most courageous man I've ever known, nor the most honest, I suppose, nor the best writer—not by far—nor the best thinker . . . though courage and honor he had in full measure, and he was a fine thinker and writer. What lifted him above his fellows was the one principle that seemed to light his life: the search for truth, his single-mindedness about that. That is the thing that elevated him and all who knew him. On his death, the unemotional Eric Severeid spoke on the air that shattering, emotional farewell of Shakespeare's.

. . . Good night, sweet prince,
And flights of angels sing thee to thy rest!

And those who knew Edward R. Murrow felt that benediction appropriate.

You will pardon me if I speak personally. I was nine or ten, and I remember my parents listening to the radio, waiting for his broadcasts from London during the war. "This is London. Early this morning, we heard the bombers going out. It was the sound of a giant factory in the sky. It seemed to shake the old gray stone buildings in this bruised and battered city beside the Thames . . ." The radio was on all the time, but when Edward R. Murrow reported from London, the kids at our house didn't talk, even if we didn't always listen.

And then I was fourteen and the winner of a schoolboy speaking and writing contest, and with my mother in a hotel room in Washington, where I had gone to receive my prize. Somebody called to say, "Be sure to listen to Murrow tonight." We did, and at the end of his broadcast there was that same voice, quoting a few lines from my speech. I met the president of the United States that same day, but when I woke up the next morning, the thing I remembered was Edward R. Murrow saying my words.

And then I was fifteen, and Ed Murrow was to make a speech in Chapel Hill. A friend called me in Charlotte to ask if I would like to come up to hear him. I sat in the audience at the Carolina Inn and I remember thinking, "Look how close I am to him, right here in the same room with him." The kind of thing a starstruck fifteen-year-old thinks. He spoke about the job ahead for television news, to develop the same kind of tradition of courage that the best newspapers had long enjoyed. Afterward my friend said, "We're taking him to the airport in the morning, would you like to come along?" So I skipped another day of high school to ride to the airport with

Edward R. Murrow. I wanted to know about London and New York and the world, but he would not speak, except to ask questions of the university student driver and—horror of horrors—of me. He questioned us in turn. So I worked in the high school newspaper, did I? What was its name? I wanted to say the *Times* or the *Herald* or the *World*, but I was forced to listen to my own voice saying, "The Rambler." Do not ask any more questions about Central High School, I remember thinking, tell us about the blitz, tell us about CBS. But he went on, looking out the window at the cotton fields that used to line the back road to the Raleigh Durham Airport, remarking that it was pretty poor-looking cotton. I thought hysterically, "Please do not spend the whole trip this way. Nobody cares about *The Rambler*, or the opinions of that kid who's driving, or that damned cotton." But that was how he spent the whole trip. I am sure he enjoyed that drive, in a passive way. But I actively hated it, was actually relieved to see him climb the steps of the plane, so as not to have to suffer any more of his questions. The student driver, by the way, who waved Mr. Murrow into his plane, was Bob Evans, who was also to become a CBS News correspondent. I went back to the car, miserable, embarrassed, wishing I had never come along, too young and inexperienced to realize that I had spent an hour with a consummate reporter who, facing an hour with nothing more to dig into than the opinions of a couple of kids and nothing more to study than the state of the cotton crop, dug into, studied, what there was at hand.

And then I was twenty-two and walking into the CBS newsroom in New York, on invitation, to talk about a job. It was just a little room—a few people working at typewriters, a bank of wire machines against the far wall. And then I saw him, from the back, in shirtsleeves, his head bent over the AP machine, unmistakably, there he was. And for me that little room became a great hall. A few minutes later an executive was offering me $135 a week to work in that room as a writer, from midnight till 8 A.M. Yes, yes, I said. I would have said yes if I had to pay them to work there.

It was hero worship, but what a hero he was! It dawned on me in the months that followed that it was not only the young, impressionable beginners who felt this way about Ed Murrow. It was everybody who knew him. "Well," he would sometimes say at the end of the day, "we have done as much damage as we can do. How about a drink?" The invitation was for everybody within the sound of his voice. And we would all go down to Colbee's on the ground floor of the CBS building, and pass an hour, the well-known correspondents and the seasoned editors and the young kids, all together, all drawn together, by Murrow. It was very nearly the best camaraderie I have ever felt, and it helped me survive in New York on $135 a week. He always bought the drinks.

There came a day when I wrote for him—an appalling idea, but that was the way radio worked. I actually wrote the news portion of his radio broadcast a few times, while he worked on the commentary. He would toss what he had written across to me to read over, while he timed and edited what I had written. Once, I found that he had written the expression "including you and I." I debated with myself before pointing out that it should be "you and me," wondering what he would say. What he said was "Good catch." It was such a little thing, all these are such little things, but it is a measure of what we all thought about Murrow that I remember to this day Murrow saying to me, "Good catch."

Well, he said other things. He wrote me notes, complimenting me on something I had done, or quarreling with something I had said on the air, or with the way I said it. He did the same for many others at CBS News, especially the young correspondents, and he did it even after he left the network. He was, until the end of his life, gracious and generous beyond all hope of explanation.

At his death, he had been director of the United States Information Agency and an adviser to presidents and prime ministers. He was holder of fourteen honorary degrees and all the prizes of his profession; honorary Knight Commander of the Order of the British Empire, Chevalier of the Legion of Honor, an officer of the Order of Leopold.

But we don't remember him for his honors. We remember him, finally, for his deep and abiding belief that we could take it; that there was never any excuse for insulating the people from reality; that escapism was the eighth and deadliest sin; that the American people were wise beyond the comprehension of those who would trick us or delude us and tell us lies; that we were decent and responsible and mature and could be counted on every time if only we could be supplied our fair measure of the straight facts.

We don't remember him for his honors. We remember him for how he honored us.

1908 Born Egbert Roscoe Murrow in N.C.—into a strictly Quaker home, where smoking, drinking, and gambling are taboo. From his father, Egbert inherits a habit of long silences.

1914 Seeking a more prosperous life in the lumber business, the Murrows move to Blanchard, Washington.

1930 By the time he has graduated from Washington State University, he has changed his name to Edward. ("If had had known how 'Egbert' looked written out, I wouldn't have given it to him," his mother says. "It doesn't look pretty.") Murrow persuades the fledgling CBS network to air *University on the Air,* interviewing luminaries like Albert Einstein.

1932 Meets Janet Brewster on a train. Marries her two years later.

1940 "This ... is London." With those trademark words, crackling over the air-waves from a city in the midst of blitzkrieg, Edward R. Murrow begins a journalistic career with no equal. Having joined CBS in the thirties, he is headquartered in London reporting on WWII. A fearless reporter who flies 20 bombing missions over Berlin (and over the objections of CBS brass), Murrow transcends the facts to offer the feel of war—commenting on what he sees in rich, visual detail. He is the first Allied correspondent to report the horrors of the Nazi death camps. (From Buchenwald: "I have reported what I saw and heard, but only part of it. For most of it I have no words. If I've offended you by this rather mild account of Buchenwald, I'm not in the least sorry.")

1943 Wins the first of four Peabody Awards. By now his name is a household word in wartime America.

1945 Returning to the U.S., Murrow is promoted to vice president of CBS News.

1950 His news documentary *See It Now* takes the public into submarines, fighter planes, even a session of the Arkansas General Assembly—setting the standard for all TV documentary shows that follow. Murrow's trademarks: an ever-present cigarette (he smokes 60-70/day), a calm baritone voice, an anxiety-ridden face.

1953 Invades the home of celebrities in gentlemanly fashion—offering profiles of stars from Sophie Tucker to Billy Graham—on *Person to Person*.

1954 Spotlights Joseph McCarthy, a damning portrait of his fanaticism that breaks his hold on America. "The actions of the junior senator from 'Wisconsin have caused alarm and dismay ... and whose fault is that? Not really his; he didn't create this situation of fear; he merely exploited it, and rather successfully. Cassius was right, 'The fault, dear Brutus, is not in our stars, but in ourselves.'"

1961 Retiring from CBS, Murrow is appointed head of the U.S. Information Agency by JFK, directing Washington's output of both news and propaganda. But three years later he is diagnosed with lung cancer and retires.

....

1965 Dies, age 57—having ushered the world into America's living rooms. His ashes are scattered at his farm in Pawling, N.Y.

....

KATHARINE GRAHAM

By Ben Bradlee, colleague and close friend

DELIVERED AT FUNERAL, JULY 23, 2001
WASHINGTON NATIONAL CATHEDRAL

What a way to go!

Lunch with Tom Hanks and Rita Wilson. Bridge with Warren Buffett and Bill Gates the day before. Dinner the night before that with admiring moguls galore, plus the new president of Mexico, and now Yo-Yo Ma, to send you on your storied way.

Not bad for the widowed mother of four, who started her career at the top, thirty-eight years ago, in great tragedy and great trepidation.

Not bad at all!

Speaking of "widowed mother of four," did you ever hear of the "Widowed Grandmother Defense," developed by our lawyers, when

Spiro T. Agnew tried to subpoena our reporters' notes in a last-ditch effort to escape jail?

We had refused to surrender the notes. Reporters don't *own* their own notes, Joe Califano told the District Court. The owner of the paper owns them. And let's see if they dare throw Katharine Graham in jail. She was delighted at the prospect.

Maybe not all of you understand what it takes to make a great newspaper. It takes a great owner. Period. An owner who commits herself with passion and the highest standards and principles to a simple search for truth. With fervor, not favor. With fairness and courage. Great owners help reporters and editors shine a bright light on the darkest corners of society.

This is what Katharine Graham brought to the table. Plus so much more . . . like a love for news, a love for answers, and love for a piece of the action.

In my memories, Katharine *always* seems to be laughing. Once during the Reagan administration we were battling the CIA, the NSA, and the White House about a story called Ivy Bells. The Russians had learned from an American spy about a super-top-secret diving bell, which we had invented to clamp onto underwater Soviet cables. As a result we knew where Soviet subs were and what they were up to.

But the Soviets had found our bell, removed it, and taken it to Moscow. The Feds were about to lose their fight to keep all of this out of the paper, when they pulled out their secret weapon, the Big Kahuna himself, the president of the United States.

Kay was in the shower when the maid knocked on the glass door to tell her, "President Reagan is on the phone. For you." My all-time favorite image of the Most Powerful Woman in the World ensued. Kay comes flying out of the shower soaking wet, grabs a towel and starts looking for a pencil and some paper. But finally she's ready. Brenda Starr, girl reporter, is at the scene, ready to go.

"Yes, Mr. President," she says, and the president starts telling her about Operation Ivy Bells, which neither one of them had ever heard of before that day. Kay takes notes furiously, until she notices that the president is repeating himself, obviously speaking from cue cards about the danger to the public if the *Post* publishes.

You all know that Katharine was a very social person. She liked exclusive clubs and fancy parties with fancy guests. But there was one small club she couldn't get into, no matter how hard she tried. It had only three members: Edward Bennett Williams, Art Buchwald, and me. And it had only one purpose: to keep other people out.

In her efforts to join the club, Kay pointed out that she had hired Williams as the *Post*'s lawyer and could fire him, that I served her at will, and that Buchwald's columns could be cancelled at any time. And she noted we had no members of the female persuasion.

But she still couldn't get in. Buchwald and Williams confided to her that I was the problem. They voted to admit her every time, they said in their suck-up voice, but I regularly blackballed her.

But on her sixty-fifth birthday, she was invited to join us for lunch. Before the soup, Buchwald announced — to my surprise — that we had at last invited her to become a member. She was thrilled, almost giddy. Until the very end of that lunch. Williams grew suddenly serious and told her the club had a sixty-five-and-out rule, and that we reluctantly had to accept her resignation. She threw her head back and guffawed.

Kay's laughter will ring in the ears of all her friends for a long time. I can hear her now, telling me she'd finally found a "much better title" for her book than I had. Mine was called *A Good Life,* and she suggested, with a smile, *A Better Life* for hers.

I can hear her wondrous laugh now when she showed me a beautiful miniature gold wringer, delicately crafted for her by an admiring dentist, after Attorney General John Mitchell had said publicly that she was going to get her you-know-what caught in a wringer if she let the *Post* keep printing stories about Watergate. And I can hear her roar some more when Art Buchwald hand-delivered a miniature gold you-know-what to go with it. She wore them proudly as charms on a plain gold necklace—at least around the office.

She even laughed when she was scared. Not really scared, but concerned about the power of some of the big shots, in whose sights we found ourselves from time to time. As in "If this is such a great story, where the hell are all the other papers?" And as in "Are we all right, because if not, don't look below."

We used to send each other Christmas letters instead of presents, and in one of these she talked about "four years of learning, of stumbling, of fun, of achievements—but especially of fun. My god, the fun. It's unfair—who else has this kind of fun?"

In another Christmas letter she said, "It's a pleasure to do business with you," which was the understatement of my lifetime.

And she closed one letter by reminding me that "the all-important thing is to continue to have fun en route. I send you a big hug, a kiss . . . and a goose."

Who ever got a better Christmas present than that?

She was a spectacular dame, and I loved her very much.

1917 Born in NYC to a businessman father and self-absorbed mother.

1933 Her father purchases a bankrupt *Washington Post* for $825,000—giving Katharine work as a copy girl and punctuating a lonely childhood with her first taste of media. At the time, the paper is the fifth paper in a five-paper town, losing $1 million/year.

1938 Graduating from University of Chicago (with neither of her parents in attendance), Katharine rejoins the *Post* a year later. "If it doesn't work, get rid of her," her father says.

1940 Marries Supreme Court law clerk Phillip Graham, who becomes publisher of the *Post.*

1961 Devastated to discover her husband's affair with a *Newsweek* staffer, she sustains an added blow: He has plans to pay her off and take complete ownership of the *Post.* She is determined not to divorce him unless he gives her controlling interest—but the issue never resolves. Mr. Graham falls into his newly diagnosed manic depression . . .

1963 . . . then commits suicide. She takes over as president of the *Post*—at a time when most women are in charge of their households and nothing else. The *Washington Post* boasts a modest circulation and more modest reputation. "I had very little idea of what I was supposed to be doing, so I set out to learn. I put one foot in front of the other, shut my eyes, and stepped off the edge."

1965 Appoints (eulogizer) Ben Bradlee as editor. They are a formidable team, heading a band of journalists that deliver plucky stories with panache.

1971 Decides to publish top-secret Pentagon Papers detailing American involvement in Vietnam. The following year, breaks Watergate story— netting the paper a Pulitzer for its coverage. Setting a new standard for investigative journalism, Graham faces down the government, supports her reporters, and wins. The paper's reputation and circulation skyrocket.

1979 Appoints first son, Donald Graham, publisher. She remains CEO and chairman—enjoying movies with Henry Kissinger, dating Adlai Stevenson, and throwing increasingly famous dinner parties in her downtime. After dinner, she prefers joining the cigar-chomping men downstairs to the polite teacup conversations upstairs.

1997 Publishes autobiography *Personal History,* which wins the Pulitzer Prize.

2001 Having guided the *Washington Post* through the historic toppling of a president, won a Pulitzer, and ruled the media scene with inimitable style, Graham dies at 84—the result of a fall. From daughter to wife to widow to woman, her rise neatly paralleled the women's movement. Graham's funeral at the Washington National Cathedral draws emissaries from every walk—political heavyweights, billionaires, and average citizens all say goodbye to the strains of Yo-Yo Ma's cello.

MALCOLM FORBES

By Steve Forbes, son

DELIVERED AT MEMORIAL SERVICE, MARCH 1, 1990
ST. BARTHOLOMEW'S CHURCH, NEW YORK CITY

My grandfather wrote in the first issue of *Forbes:* "Business was originated to produce happiness, not to pile up millions." By that criterion, my father was truly a rich man. As he once wrote, "I'll be the saddest one at my funeral."

What made his happiness so precious and unique, so contagious and convincing, was that he knew all too well the hurts and disappointments of life.

He was no stranger to physical pain. A machine gunner in the army during World War II, he was seriously wounded and spent almost a year recovering in various military hospitals. When he talked about this, which was rare, it was with jocular anecdotes about various ways he tried to scratch his back when in a cast. A little over a decade ago, he came down with a form of cancer that had a high mortality rate. For two years, he underwent painful treatments. Only those closest to him knew he had the disease, and to us he never complained.

These, and other experiences he had, including serious injuries from several motorcycle and balloon accidents, can harden people. With Pop, they simply deepened his already considerable empathy for others who suffer.

Nor was he a stranger to adversity and setbacks, personal and professional. His divorce from Mother after thirty-nine years of marriage almost shattered him. As can happen, they loved each other but found it impossible to live together.

When growing up, Pop's burning ambition was to enter politics and become president of the United States. He pursued this goal with customary zeal. But by the age of forty, his political hopes were in ruins; he recognized he wasn't going to make it. So he turned his formidable energies to the magazine and elsewhere.

He had his share of business setbacks. His attempt to start a chain of weekly newspapers in Ohio after graduating from college went nowhere, a venture that was mercifully cut short by U.S. entry into the Second World War. In the late 1940s, he had high hopes for a hardbound magazine he launched called *Nation's Heritage*. As he put it, "I spent so much money on the production that I had little left over for promotion." He never made that mistake again.

He was also no stranger to the underside of human nature. No one who served in combat as he did could escape it. There were numerous times when his trust in others was not reciprocated.

Yet for all this, which so often sours so many of us as we get older, he never lost his almost childlike capacity to wonder, to be curious, to dream, and to do. His buoyant, infectious spirit of openness, of generosity, of let's-try-it was always with him.

When he was dealt a setback, he would initially look as if he had been physically hit by a punch. He would take stock—and then move ahead as if nothing had happened. When he did look back on disappointments, it was always with good-natured humor. His failure to win the governorship of New Jersey, for instance: "I was nosed out by a landslide."

He was incapable of ill will or of pining for what might have been. Grudges and grievances were never a part of this man's makeup. He genuinely believed that things turned out for the best.

He was generous. As a parent, he had unbounded love for his children and his grandchildren. He gave away much money to many causes. In a great number of cases, the recipient never knew who was the benefactor. He wanted to share his numerous collections with others. He thought it would be "neat" if people could see what turned him on about these items. But he didn't want a mere display. When he looked at a toy boat, for instance, he also saw waves and movement. This sense of life and motion is reflected in the galleries here at 60 Fifth Avenue, which have been visited by tens of thousands.

As I was given greater responsibility, I became ever more impressed with his generosity with two particularly valuable commodities: his time and his authority. His office door was rarely closed. Anyone and everyone could and did stop in. Only when dictating editorials did he resent an intrusion. If he needed uninterrupted time, he simply came in at the wee hours of the morning.

He never hoarded his power like a miser. He took delight in delegating authority to those he felt had earned it. To him, that was smart business—their success meant more success for the company.

He loved people. People sensed this and were quickly at ease with him. He never tried to make himself look bigger by making others feel smaller.

What was he like as a father? Looking back, I can only hope I do half as well with my children as he did with us.

Perhaps because he always had something of the child in him, he knew instinctively how to nurture and bring out the adult in us as we grew up. When I was nine years old, I wanted a shotgun and to learn how to shoot skeet. My father had had an abhorrence of weapons of any type since the war. He certainly wasn't going to let me take something like this up at such a young age. I persisted, and for Christmas I received a 20-gauge Beretta. He made sure that I learned to use it safely. He emphasized to me what his father had emphasized to him, "With possessions, son, come responsibilities."

When I was fifteen, the Surgeon General's first report on the dangers of smoking came out. My father was then consuming up to four packs a day. He immediately stopped and never took it up again. At the time, I was experimenting with cigarettes. Like most of my peers, I assumed that cigarette smoking was part of becoming an adult. My father said to me, "I'm not going to tell you not to smoke. I'm asking you not to do it." He promised no reward, as many other parents did, if I resisted the temptation. "You should do it for the sake of your health." The manner in which he made his request made this adolescent feel, as the cliché goes, like a man, and I never puffed a cigarette again.

When I went to work at the magazine, I did so with some trepidation. I had read too many stories about the difficulties of a son working for his father. My worries were misplaced. He was never overbearing, never tried to micromanage my work. "I have my own way of doing things and, in time, you will develop yours," he told me then. "Don't try to be what you're not; you'll only send yourself to an early grave." He was quick to praise; his infrequent criticisms were almost always on target and always given with the intent to help, not hurt.

A couple of years after I went to work, I began to write editorials for the magazine. Inevitably, I would occasionally want to express opinions that differed rather sharply from his. He would argue with me, but if I stuck to my guns, he would smile and shake his head: "Okay, it's your name that's on this." Occasionally, he would say, "You've convinced me. I've changed my mind." I would be on the clouds for the rest of the week. His philosophy was to allow me, and eventually my brothers, enough latitude to learn from our mistakes, but not to be destroyed by them.

No matter what he did, no matter how impressive the achievement in business, ballooning, writing, motorcycling, entertaining, and collecting, we knew that as long as he lived, the best was always yet to come. Now he is gone. But in a larger, truer sense, death has not triumphed, and if we follow, as he did, the better angels of our nature, it never will.

1919 Born in Brooklyn, N.Y., the third son of a Scottish immigrant who founded *Forbes* magazine.

1941 Graduates from Princeton and heads for the army. Serving in Europe, he is wounded and eventually discharged with a Purple Heart.

1954 Takes over *Forbes* upon his father's death.

1957 Unsuccessfully runs for N.J. governor. Rededicating himself to the magazine, Forbes becomes editor and publisher, buying out his family. Under his leadership, the publication flourishes—promoting the values of laissez-faire capitalism, and famous for its roundup of the 400 wealthiest Americans. Forbes's own lifestyle is legendary: His private jet *Capitalist Tool*, "Highlander" yacht, huge art collections including nine Fabergé eggs, French Chateau de Balleroy, and sprawling Colorado ranch fuel his colorful, high-rolling image.

1974 Makes the first free flight over Beijing in a hot-air balloon. Goes on to set six world records in ballooning.

1985 After divorcing Roberta, wife of 39 years, he is frequently seen in the company of Elizabeth Taylor, and astride motorcycles.

1989 Spends $5 million celebrating his 70th birthday—a characteristically lavish two-day affair in Morocco, accented with fireworks and dancing through the night. A thousand guests usher Forbes into his eighth decade. After the party, Forbes is declared an honorary citizen of Tangier.

1990 The colorful publisher and unabashed salesman for capitalism dies, age 70, with a net worth of at least $400 million. At his funeral, a lone bagpiper gives rise to the rolling thunder of motorcycle engines as leather-clad bikers gun their engines in salute. Having coined the phrase, "He who dies with the most toys wins," Forbes is cremated and his ashes interred at his private island in Fiji.

DAVID BRINKLEY

By Joel Brinkley, son

DELIVERED AT FUNERAL, JUNE 16, 2003
OAKDALE CEMETERY, WILMINGTON, NORTH CAROLINA

My father led a charmed life. He is the only person I have ever known, the only one, who always said and did precisely what he wanted, when he wanted, no matter the consequences. And for eighty-two years, more often than not, it served him well. As I said, he led a charmed life.

But his life was a paradox. I have never met a man so utterly sure of himself, so supremely confident—to the point that he once calmly advised me: "You know, a little bit of arrogance is not such a bad thing." And when a reporter sat down to interview him for a profile or some other story, I so often heard him say: Ask me any question you want, any question. I don't care." And he didn't.

The incongruity was that he was also an exceedingly private man—self-contained, uncaring what the world had to say about him. Never boastful, never self-promotional. Far from it, which is why all of us are here instead of climbing out of limousines in front of the national cathedral.

Now and then when I was a boy, we would be walking some place in public and somebody would stop him, eyes aglow, and ask: "Aren't you, aren't you . . . Chet Huntley?"

Dad would smile, his face perfectly composed, and he would say: "Yes. Nice to see you," and walk on. One time when that happened I asked him: "Dad, why did you do that?" He shrugged and he said, "It doesn't really matter, and this way it's over quicker and nobody's embarrassed."

Years later, when he retired in 1997, my employer, the *New York Times,* gave me an odd assignment. The executive editor asked me to write a profile of my father. So I called Dad and asked what he thought of this idea. His answer was immediate and genuine.

"There's no story here," he said. "I don't know why you'd want to do it."

That was not false modesty. It was his secret. He didn't matter. That's what he thought, and that is also how he regarded the self-important kings, presidents, potentates and, particularly, the members of Congress he covered for fifty years. None of you are really as important as you would have us believe. He regarded them as if he were a bemused uncle. That's how he covered them. That was his charm.

It's hard to imagine how any father could have been a more powerful mentor than my father was to us. I credit my father with giving me the independence, the self-confidence, to make a go of it in the world. That's not to say he did not help. When I tried to start out in journalism thirty years ago, as I was getting ready to graduate from college, up the road at the University of North Carolina,

I applied to dozens of newspapers but couldn't get a job. I tacked the rejection letters to the wall. They reached to the ceiling.

But then one day Dad called and told me: "I heard there might be a job at the Associated Press in Charlotte." That's all he said. I wondered where he had heard this. But the next day I drove over to Charlotte. And yes, they offered me a job. Night radio, writing briefs on the dedication of the new firehouse in Florence, South Carolina.

It wasn't much, but it was a start. And after that he stayed out of the way. I was on my own. But just a few years ago, long after I had started working for the *Times*, I ran into my former boss at the Associated Press. Only then did he tell me that in forty years, the general manager of the Associated Press — the chief executive — had never once called the Charlotte bureau for anything, ever — until the day he called to tell them to hire me.

Dad had arranged it. He never told me.

Now he is gone — though not entirely. David Brinkley left his unmistakable stamp on the world of television news — the world he helped to create.

But he also left his strong imprint, elements of his character, on all of us — his children.

None of us is able to carry it as coolly, as gracefully as he did — which just goes to demonstrate what all of us know. My father was a singular individual. A treasure. The nation will miss him. And the Lord knows, so will we.

1920 Born in Wilmington, N.C.

1936 Writes for the *Wilmington Morning Star* while still in high school. His column is "full of such racy items as who was buying 10-cent sodas for whom," Brinkley later says, "each one separated by three dots."

1938 Attends North Carolina, Emory, and Vanderbilt universities but leaves minus a degree because "I didn't think there was anything they could teach me."

1943 Discharged from the army, Brinkley moves to Washington and takes a job as NBC's first White House correspondent.

1945 First appears on air in the news show *America United*.

1946 Marries Ann Fischer. They have two children.

1956 Looking for their own star to compete with CBS's Walter Cronkite, NBC is torn between Chet Huntley and David Brinkley—finally deciding on both. The two anchor NBC's newscast from NYC and Washington, Brinkley's dry wit punctuating Huntley's serious tone. *The Huntley-Brinkley Report* quickly becomes America's favorite newscast, lasting 14 years and setting the standard for TV journalism. Brinkley's explanation of success: "I wrote pretty well, and Huntley looked good and had a great voice."

1964 The program sets the pace for TV news. Their coverage of the Democratic Convention draws an astounding 84% viewership.

1970 When Huntley retires, the show is rechristened *NBC Nightly News*. Brinkley becomes commentator.

1981 On the heels of several critically acclaimed but lesser newsmagazine shows, Brinkley leaves NBC—a "rending, wrenching experience" that brings tears to his eyes. Almost immediately, ABC offers him *This Week with David Brinkley*—an opinionated roundtable discussion that proves highly successful.

1992 Wins the Peabody Award for his report on Pearl Harbor.

1996 Retires from *This Week*, then surprises the media by taking a job as spokesperson for an agricultural behemoth. ABC pulls, then reinstates, the ads.

2003 Dies at 82 in his Houston home, after "doing the news longer than any-one on earth." A legend known for his clipped voice and and dry wit—mimicked by anchors and comics alike—he wrote an autobiography whose subtitle is his news legacy: *11 Presidents, 4 Wars, 22 Political Conventions, 1 Moon Landing, 3 Assassinations, 2,000 Weeks of News, and Other Stuff on Television and 18 Years of Growing Up in North Carolina.* Unmentioned: 10 Emmys, three Peabodys, and the Presidential Medal of Freedom.

HENRY LUCE

By Robert T. Elson, Time *colleague*

WRITTEN IN COMMEMORATION

On the last Friday that he was in the office, Harry Luce was having lunch with a half dozen top editors of *Time.* No sooner had they finished ordering than he began to pull from his pockets articles torn from the Phoenix papers. The questions began, rapid-fire. Was there a story for *Time* in this one? What was behind the transfer of the Air Force general from the National Air College? Shouldn't we be doing something more about Rhodesia? The editors looked at each other and smiled. It was like old times; Harry Luce was at work suggesting, asking, prodding.

He resigned his title of editor in chief in 1964 because he said he wanted to take things a little easier. He never did, really. He was as deeply interested and involved in what the magazines were reporting and what was going on in the world around him as before. But there were some differences. Phoenix gave him a sense of detachment and a little different perspective. His schedule was less crowded; his desk was in his bedroom and he worked at his convenience. In the afternoon, attended by his favorite caddy, Andy, who always improved the lies, he usually played nine rounds of golf. He was never idle. From Phoenix the daily mail brought to the thirty-fourth floor a stream of letters, memos, clippings.

When the news broke on Tuesday morning that—as *Time* used to say when he edited the magazine—death, as it must to all men, came to Henry Robinson Luce, there was shock, then a sense of personal grief and loss. But it was softened in the corridors and offices of Time Incorporated as the memories came flooding back.

From his earliest school days in China, Harry Luce wanted to be a journalist, and a journalist he was all his life. He once told how, during his senior year at Yale, Dr. Amos Wilder, father of his friend and classmate Thornton Wilder, pled with him to abandon his ambition: "Harry, don't go into journalism," said Dr. Wilder. "It will turn you into a cynic and corrupt and corrode you. It will turn your wine into vinegar. You will lose your soul."

In years later, Luce said, "To the extent that I have become corrupted and corroded I cannot blame it on journalism. Partly because I had good luck and had no reason to become sour and cynical about my profession, and partly because the climate of journalism changed." Luce himself, of course, had a large part in changing that climate. When he went to work on the *Chicago Daily News* in the twenties, "journalist" was a word held to scorn by the cynical newspapermen of that day. Luce once said, "I have sometimes said to myself that the one thing I was determined to do was to make 'journalist' a good word, and today it is a good word."

No one who worked for him will forget his questions. They were often disconcerting but never irrelevant. "I discovered what a magnificent editor he could be," said Archibald MacLeish, the poet and dramatist who was one of *Fortune*'s original writers. "Harry would ask the simple question that most editors would be ashamed to ask, and it would blow the whole thing up—the question that cried out to be asked." A lady seated next to Luce at a dinner was startled to be asked: "What do you think of the resurrection of the body?" He was entirely serious; he wanted to know how a professed church member interpreted this article of the Nicene Creed.

On his way to interview the emperor of Japan, he asked his companion to help him frame an unusual question: how would you ask the emperor how it felt to be a mortal and no longer revered as a god? Luce found a way to frame the question without impertinence, but at this point the Imperial interpreter's English failed him.

As an editor he was constantly making suggestions. When the managing editor apologized for failing to heed one, Luce replied, "Don't ever worry about ignoring my story suggestions. . . . Well, I realize that they are made without benefit of a systematic knowledge of all the story possibilities. . . . Certainly they always are offered to aid rather than to harass!"

Luce's memos are cherished by those who received them. They varied greatly in length: from four famous words—"See me about Hitler"—to nineteen closely reasoned pages on "The Principles, Policies, Attitudes, Etc. Which Govern and Motivate Time Inc." He addressed another one to the publisher of *Fortune* years ago in answer to criticism of a series on U.S. Steel: "Every time we tell a good story we are right, or every time we tell a right story we are good— that is a damn funny thing about journalism. All the troubles are when the stories aren't very good or very right.

"Ditto with *Time.*

"Ditto with *Life.*"

His proudest moments, he said, on any number of occasions, were when he stood as editor in chief before a company of Time Inc.-ers. Many years ago he started the custom of sending out a silver porringer to newborn members of the Time Inc. family; thousands have now been given in his name. He was touched one Christmas by a letter from a member of the staff who told him what his employment at Time Incorporated had meant; he listed the house that he owned, the children he had educated. Luce circulated this to a small group with the question, "How do you answer this letter?" Briton Hadden and Luce very early made it possible for their small staff to buy stock in the company; when the company grew bigger, Luce inaugurated profit-sharing. When one of his associates one day rather fatuously suggested that he was treating him and his associates too generously, Luce turned on him and said, "Why? Do you want to be poor? I was poor once and I saw no merit in it if you can honestly avoid it."

Luce did not set great store by possessions; his pictures were good but it was not a great collection. His coffee and night tables usually contained the latest books on public affairs and religion; but Mr. and Mrs. Luce also devoured murder mysteries. He liked them for the same reason he liked jigsaw puzzles; the latest and most difficult puzzle was usually laid out on a card table.

In his earlier years, Luce played tennis moderately well; in recent years, golf, but never very seriously. "The wonderful world of sport"—a phrase which he coined—never seriously interested him until the coming of *Sports Illustrated,* which was a favorite of his as the youngest in the family. Actually Luce never irrevocably proclaimed a favorite magazine, and liked everyone to guess; each editor had reason to consider his magazine the favorite in some particular way.

The cause to which Harry Luce dedicated his life and these magazines was his country, but his patriotism was not the "My country right or wrong" brand. Having been born in China of missionary parents and having not seen his own country until he was seven years old, he once said: "In some ways that background endowed me with special qualifications to be editor in chief, in some ways it disqualified me. First of all, I gained a too romantic, too idealistic view of America. This came from the fact that the Americans I grew up with—all of them—were good people. I had no experience of evil in terms of Americans. Put along with that the idea that America was a wonderful country, with opportunity and freedom and justice for all, and you get not only an idealistic but a romantic view—a profoundly false romantic view. I was never disillusioned with or by America, but I was, from my earliest manhood, dissatisfied with America. America was not being as great and as good as I knew she could be, as I believe with every nerve and fiber God himself had intended her to be."

1898 Born in China to missionary parents, the first of four children. His father's religious impulses take root in "Harry," who writes sermons for diversion.

1908 Attends Chefoo School for the next five years—where students are routinely caned. Learns Chinese before English.

1913 Attending school in Conn., he fatefully meets Briton Hadden. They edit the school newspaper. Sharing a passion for journalism and a belief that the ignorant public ought to be enlightened, they carry their partnership all the way to Yale, editing the *Yale Daily News.*

1920 Voted "Most Brilliant," Luce graduates from Yale and continues studies at Oxford. Returns the following year for a job with *Chicago Daily News.*

1923 Raising $100,000 seed money, he and Hadden launch *Time.* With short articles summarizing important events and issues, and a strong POV, the magazine pledges "a prejudice against the rising cost of government; faith in the things which money cannot buy, a respect for the old, particularly in manners." Marries Lila Hotz.

A Wonderful Life

1927 *Time* sells 175,000 copies/week.

1929 Hadden dies and Luce assumes ownership of Time, Inc. A man of missionary zeal and limitless curiosity, he expands his publishing repertoire with *Fortune* magazine—followed by *Life* (1936), *House and Home* (1952), and *Sports Illustrated* (1954). Unabashedly straightforward—a staunch Republican, foe of big labor, and defender of big business—Luce encourages his editors to choose a side. "Show me a man who claims he is objective, and I'll show you a man with illusions."

1934 Meets Clare Boothe Brokaw, editor at *Vanity Fair*. The following year, he divorces Lila and marries Clare.

1942 Clare is elected U.S. Congresswoman, the first of two terms.

1953 Clare is appointed U.S. ambassador to Italy by Eisenhower. Luce sets up offices in Rome, communicating with his staff by memos—of which he is a prolific composer. His editor in chief explains, "The long ones are neatly typewritten. The others consist of pencil scrawls on yellow pad paper, often with a newspaper clipping attached by means of an ordinary straight pin."

1964 Luce retires as editor in chief of Time, Inc. Started on a shoestring $86,000, his empire is now worth $500 million—with magazines spanning 13 editions and a world circulation of 13 million copies/issue.

1967 Dies of a heart attack, age 68—having created the modern news magazine, influenced the tastes and conversations of millions, while remaining a largely private man who "lived well above the tree line on Olympus," as one of his editors remembered.

ENTERTAINERS

FRED ROGERS

By Teresa Heinz, longtime friend

DELIVERED AT MEMORIAL SERVICE, MAY 3, 2003
PITTSBURGH, PENNSYLVANIA

Saying goodbye to friends is always hard. But saying goodbye to a man whose character defined friendship for generations of children and adults is so much harder. Fred was godfather to my son Christopher. He was my good friend and, during summers on Nantucket, quite literally my neighbor.

But for Fred, the whole world was his neighbor, and everyone his friend. So I am keenly aware that I speak now not just for me, but also for millions who grieve the loss of this special man.

I once asked Fred which of the characters he most identified with in his world of make-believe. "Daniel Tiger," he told me. For those of you who don't remember, Daniel is painfully shy. You might wonder how Fred could have been shy and yet become so famous that he was nothing short of a cultural icon. The answer is simple: magic. But his was not the magic of illusionists or the trickery of entertainers. It was the simple magic of love.

Fred once shared with me a letter that he received from the mother of an autistic boy. Every day her son would watch *Mister Rogers' Neighborhood*. And when the program was done and the television was turned off, the boy would stand up from his chair and try to talk or sing about what he had seen. But his language was garbled and no one could understand his words. Then one day, when the boy was five, he stood up from his chair as always and started singing. But this day his words were unmistakable: "It's a wonderful day in the neighborhood."

It was a small miracle, perhaps, the breaking of a barrier, the opening of a life. But Fred gave so many people similar gifts, and he did it merely by speaking to them in an open, honest, nonthreatening way. He never condescended—he just invited us into a conversation. He spoke to us as the people we were, not as the people he wished we were.

That simple gift of acceptance made him one of the most trusted and powerful men I have ever known. When my late husband, John, was sworn in as a U.S. Senator in 1976, Fred was there as our guest and next to him sat a little boy. He greeted Fred: "Hello, Mr. Rogers." They exchanged introductions and then the boy launched into the most horribly gruesome story about the death of his pet goat. It was an odd story to tell a stranger, full of gore and blood. But to this boy, Fred was no stranger. Mr. Rogers was someone he could trust, someone who could console him, and that is precisely what Fred did.

In his work Fred told the story of *all* our feelings. He showed children the real world—that universe of people and places he shared with them from his kitchen table, sitting there in his sneakers and sweater. And he showed them the world of make-believe, the land of King Friday and H. J. Elephant, whom he named for my late husband. That line between reality and make-believe is so often blurred in our society, and it isn't a kind gift to our children, creating as it does so many false expectations. Fred honored the need that children have for a real world they can feel safe in, a make-believe world they can escape to, and the ability to tell the difference.

Fred was able to look past the differences that so often are all we see in each other in this life. He focused instead on what all of us— children and adult, black and white, Christian and Jew, Muslim and nonbeliever—have in common: the need to feel special, to be accepted for who and what we are. What a gift that was, and how wise we would be to hold on to it in this newly conflicted world of ours, this global neighborhood.

I'm so sorry that Fred has left us. But I am so grateful that he blessed us with his life. His work will continue beyond this point. *Mister Rogers' Neighborhood* will continue to air on public television. His production company will carry on, as he wished. But most of all, every one of us whose lives he touched will continue to hold his gentle yet strong spirit deep inside of us.

This summer I will bike over to the Crooked House in Madaket, the lovely beach cottage where Fred composed and wrote so much. There, beside the lapping water, I am sure I will find Elvira, his high priestess of seagulls, with her loud congregation of gulls flapping overhead. I will sit in the sand and take in their song, the song of Fred's life, and let it envelop me in a reverie that will never go away. We all have a place like that, a place that symbolizes Fred, this dear friend of ours.

Let us remember him there.

A Wonderful Life

1928 Born in Latrobe, Pa.

1930 An only child until age 11, when his parents adopt, Fred spends large amounts of time with his puppets.

1951 Graduates from Rollins College with a degree in music. Transfixed by the possibilities of TV, he gets a job as a gofer at NBC, working his way up to floor director of shows like *Your Hit Parade.*

1952 Marries college sweetheart Joanne Byrd.

1953 Returns to Pittsburgh to develop *The Children's Corner,* the nation's first public television program. Rogers is off-screen puppeteer, introducing Daniel Striped Tiger, King Friday XIII, Lady Elaine Fairchilde, and Curious X the Owl. On lunch breaks he studies theology at a nearby seminary.

1959 James Rogers is born—the first of two children.

1963 Ordained a Presbyterian minister.

1968 *Mister Rogers' Neighborhood* debuts on PBS. With none of the animation and fizz of *Sesame Street,* the show is openly dedicated to teaching children to love themselves—addressing childhood fears in song and skit. Rogers: "I got into television because I hated it so. And I thought there was some way of using this fabulous instrument to be of nurture to those who would watch and listen." Guests find Rogers, who writes and produces all shows, a perfectionist unwilling to let half-baked ad-libs go on the air.

1971 Forms his production company, Family Communications, Inc.

1976 His car is stolen. When the thieves discover it belongs to Mister Rogers, they return the station wagon with sincere apologies.

1981 Eddie Murphy parodies Rogers on *Saturday Night Live* as the black "Mr. Robinson," lamenting, "I hope I get to move into your neighborhood some day. The problem is that when I move in, y'all move away." The skit earns Rogers' admiration and all but ensures his place in pop culture.

1983 Receives a Peabody Award for "25 beautiful years in the neighborhood." Pens the first of five books, *Mister Rogers Talks with Parents*.

1984 The Smithsonian adds Rogers's sweater to its permanent collection.

1990 Sues the Ku Klux Klan, forcing them to stop playing racist telephone recordings imitating his voice and theme song.

2001 Last original episodes of *Mister Rogers' Neighborhood* air on PBS.

2002 Rogers keeps a busy schedule outside the Neighborhood: Receives the Presidential Medal of Freedom. Gives a commencement speech at Dartmouth. And films public service announcements advising parents how to handle the first anniversary of 9/11.

2003 Dies of stomach cancer, age 74—the thoughtful neighbor whose heart-to-heart talks with children taught them how to get along in the world.

BOB HOPE

By Larry Gelbart, friend, former Hope writer

DELIVERED AT MEMORIAL SERVICE, AUGUST 27, 2003
ST. CHARLES BORROMEO CHURCH, TOLUCA LAKE, CALIFORNIA

Given that each of us stems from a fairly common cocktail of chromosomes and genes, what is it then that distinguishes us, each of us from the other? Why are a select few blessed with the spark of individuality that allows him or her to stand out from the crowd? Today, we celebrate a man who not only stood out in that way; his very presence was often why a crowd had gathered in the first place.

Whatever its source, the spark that ignited and fueled Bob Hope's life was one of such intensity—its flame so insistent—it sustained him for a full century.

And he made it all seem so easy, Bob did. So seemingly effortless to be so entertaining. So confident. So winning. So in charge.

He was always at the top of his game, his timing never less than impeccable.

Onstage. Backstage. On no stage at all.

Always prepared he was, this man for four hundred seasons.

Always ready for any situation, in any social configuration, be it a one-on-one encounter or one that was one-on-thousands, or as was so often the case with Bob, one that was one-on-millions. Always as ready to seize an opportunity as he was adept at creating new ones, Bob defied you to take your eyes off him. Or your ears. He had a personality that no lens could resist, and a hypnotic, forceful projection that made it seem as though he was amplified from within.

Yet standing in his favorite place—before any camera anywhere at all—or turning yet one more microphone into a trophy, at his most revealed, at his most public, some part of him seemed forever held in reserve. Some part of Bob that was perhaps judging us, all the while we thought we were judging him.

Consider the altogether appropriateness of his name. A name that consisted of two verbs.

Given the all but perpetual state of his motion, far from being an Everyman, Bob was, in truth, an Everywhereman. From start to finish of a career without parallel, the speed with which he created a mosaic of accomplishments suggests that his latter years perhaps offered him the first time in his kudo-crammed life in which he ever allowed himself to catch his breath.

Asked at eighty-six why he didn't retire and go fishing, Bob's reply was: "Fish don't applaud."

And so he worked as hard to win the applause of his last audiences as he did those out front in his youthful, embryonic days in vaudeville, where the apprentice legend did everything from delivering songs and snappy patter, to tripping the light fantastic, literally fantastic, entwined in the multiplicity of arms that belonged to his lovely dancing partners, Daisy and Violet Hilton—a set of Siamese twins.

There's no question that Bob amused us as much as he did because he was so amused himself.

Amused by sham. Amused by pretense. Especially when either of those failings happened to be his own. Amused by the vanity and foolishness that is the specialty of our species, he acted as a kind of cruise director of the same boat that we all find ourselves in.

He shunned sentimentality. Mocked it, in fact. This was not a king's jester, hiding a heart full of disappointments. This was the king of jesters, whose aim it was to help us get over ours. Like the best of his breed, Bob knew that life without laughter is life without parole. And the ability to provide that laughter was forever at the tip of his fingers—to say nothing of his tongue.

When the occasion arose (at the rate of say, fifty times a day), Bob's mind was quick enough to scan his memory, with the speed of a computer, to locate and deliver a joke that he might have first told decades and decades earlier. At the same time he was nimble and creative enough to come up with an altogether new line. One that was completely original.

Completely apt. Completely on target.

It was that uncanny ability of what went on constantly under Bob's straw hat—or his golf cap—or his helmet liner—to make dialog that was specially written for him sound as though it was completely spontaneous conversation.

Conversely, his delivery was such, he often made his true, spontaneous conversation sound as though it was dialog that had been specially written for him. Energized by curiosity and endless interests, powered by a playful restlessness, Bob's mind was a wonderful place to be invited to visit.

Did he need writers? people were forever asking.

Not to write his own life, he didn't. For somehow, over time, a seamless blending occurred, wherein Bob's personal and professional styles merged where, by some personal alchemy, they seemed to become one and the same.

It was not so much a case of life imitating art as it was turning art into a life.

The one in which Bob got to construct the plot. The one in which he got to call all the shots. So often called upon to play the cowardly loser, in the larger movie that was his life, the one called *The Road to Immortality,* there was a true gallantry about him. And he was the winningest loser imaginable.

In his movies, Bob rarely, if ever, got the girl he hoped to get. In his personal scenario, Bob arranged to get just the girl he wanted. The one he held on to until the very last reel.

As material and lore about him continues to be gathered—as his life continues to be a legacy-in-progress—I'm often asked to recall a favorite anecdote, some amusing occurrence that took place during the days I spent working with him.

It was, in truth, one long anecdote that lasted four delightful years. The man himself was a walking anecdote.

Pressed for something that won't take quite that long to retell, I repeat a telegram he once sent to a secretary of his, a young woman who had just been married. The message, which Bob had delivered to the bride in her honeymoon suite, consisted of only two words of advice. The two words? "Act surprised."

"Act surprised." "Fish don't applaud." Brevity, indeed, is the soul of wit.

And so, indeed, was Bob Hope.

A Wonderful Life

1903 Born Leslie Townes Hope in London, England—the fifth of seven children. Later jokes this is how he learned to dance: standing in line for the bathroom.

1908 The Hopes come to America, settling in Cleveland, Ohio.

1920 Dropping out of high school, Hope changes his name to "Packy East" during a brief stint as a boxer, before settling on "Bob." His big break arrives four years later when he opens for Fatty Arbuckle—launching him onto the vaudeville circuit.

1933 Marries Grace Louise Troxell, his vaudeville partner of five years. They divorce within months.

1934 Marries Dolores DeFina, a Bronx-born nightclub singer. They go on to adopt four children, and remain together until his death—holding the record for the longest Hollywood marriage, 69 years.

1936 Cast in Cole Porter's *It's De-Lovely,* Hope ad-libs to everyone's delight but costar Ethel Merman's. "If that so-called comedian ever behaves like that again," she threatens, "I'll use my shoe to remodel his ski nose."

1938 Rolls out his signature song *Thanks for the Memory.*

1940 A banner year: Makes *The Road to Singapore,* the first of seven road movies with Bing Crosby and Dorothy Lamour. Their breezy, ad-libbed repartee rockets the film to No. 1. Wins an Academy Award—the first of four—for his contributions to film. And his radio show is the top-rated broadcast in the US.

1942 Launches the first of many USO tours—eventually spanning six decades and 11 million anxious soldiers. Decades later he tours Vietnam and the Persian Gulf, playing to the sons of soldiers he'd entertained earlier.

1950 Hope slows his film career—only to spark a new medium. A televised Christmas special begins an exclusive relationship with NBC that delivers 285 specials.

1960 Quipping, "Golf is my real profession—showbiz pays my green fees," he founds the Bob Hope Golf Classic.

1963 JFK presents him with the Presidential Gold Medal in recognition of his "services to the country." Hope responds: "I feel very humble but I think I have the strength of character to fight it."

1985 Receives the Lifetime Achievement Award from the Kennedy Center.

1997 Honors pile on: The U.S. Navy dedicates the USNS *Bob Hope*. Congress proclaims Hope an honorary veteran. And *The Guinness Book of World Records* cites Hope as the most honored entertainer in the world— having received more than 50 honorary doctorates, and thousands of awards.

2003 Privately celebrates his 100th birthday, joking "I'm so old, they've cancelled my blood type." Later he contracts pneumonia. On his deathbed, his wife asks where he wants to be buried. Having made an art and a vast fortune out of the one-line gag, Hope responds: "Surprise me."

JOHN BELUSHI

By Dan Aykroyd, creative partner and longtime friend

DELIVERED AT MEMORIAL SERVICE, MARCH 11, 1982
CATHEDRAL OF ST. JOHN THE DIVINE, NEW YORK CITY

I wrote many things for and with John. I know this is one assignment he'd rather I didn't have to take on. Although I had a close, head-to-head, arm-to-arm, working relationship with John, that proximity never affected the fact that from the moment I met him, through all the work, I remained his number one fan. He was a brilliant performer, writer, tactician, business strategist and, most important, he was the only man I could dance with.

He was a great—a world-class—emissary of American humor. John was a patriot, a resident of the most wide-open, liberal society on earth, and he took full advantage of it. In some cases, real greatness gives license for real indulgence; whether it's as a reward, as therapy, or as sanctuary. For as hard as John worked, there had to be an additional illicit thrill to make the effort all the more worthwhile.

John was a nighthawk, true, but he was not an immoral individual. He was a good man, a kind man, a warm man, a *hot* man. What we are talking about here is a good man and a *bad boy*.

John visited me in Canada one summer. He was, naturally, allowed to cross the Canadian border without having one piece of identification. He rarely carried ID. He didn't have to. First of all, his word was good, his handshake honored, and he was the kind of guy you just wanted to give to. All the doors on the continent were open to John. He would walk into the homes of complete strangers—I watched it happen and I heard a number of stories about it—go into the kitchen, open the refrigerator, have a sandwich, turn on the TV and go to sleep on the couch while the lucky home-dwellers watched in amazement and delight. I once told him, and he liked it, that he was America's guest. And he hadn't yet worn out his welcome.

The first blues number we ever performed was a song called "King Bee." Although John hated being a bee, he didn't mind it under those circumstances because he was able to be the King Bee.

Last summer on the Vineyard, John was the happiest I'd ever seen him. We were out one morning in his Jeep and I played an instrumental by the Ventures on the tape deck. He asked me what it was called. I told him. He laughed, I laughed, and we promised each other that we'd force it upon a churchful of people at the time of our respective deaths. Whoever went first.

So here it is, for the King Bee, a little closer by the Ventures, called the "2000-Pound Bee."

[Music plays.]

A Wonderful Life

1949 Born John Adam Belushi, in Chicago, Ill.

1967 Athletic and artistic, Belushi takes to the football field (nickname: Killer Belushi) and the stage. As a Nazi camp counselor in a variety show, he catches the eye of Judith Jacklin, and they become sweethearts.

1970 Graduates from Dupage Junior College.

1971 Disregarding his father's offer to manage the family restaurant, Belushi auditions for Second City comedy troupe, and at 22 becomes their youngest member. Proceeds to steal scenes. His comic style teeters on dangerous ground—exploiting violence and social upheaval as a source of humor. Begins experimenting with drugs.

1975 Moves to New York City to become part of a new sketch comedy group known as *Saturday Night Live*. Cast includes Chevy Chase, Dan Aykroyd, and Gilda Radner. On January 17, 1976, dons a bee costume and utters, "I'm a king bee, buzzing around your hive."

1976 Marries Judith Jacklin.

1978 Stars in *National Lampoon's Animal House* as beer-guzzling fraternity goof—launching a nationwide collegiate craze for toga parties. Life follows suit: Eating, drinking, drugging—all increase proportionately as his star rises.

1979 After four seasons, Belushi and Aykroyd quit *Saturday Night Live* to try new venues.

1980 The duo star in *The Blues Brothers*. Stardom continues, as does Belushi's drug use.

1982 Chateau Marmount, Bungalow 3: Deciding to experiment, Belushi shoots up a speed ball—the mix of heroin and cocaine causes complete respiratory failure. Belushi dies at the age of 34.

WALT DISNEY

By Roy Disney, brother

WRITTEN IN COMMEMORATION

Not long ago at our Burbank studio, a group of animators and writers were holding a story conference on a new Disney cartoon feature. They were having a tough time agreeing on a story line, and the atmosphere was as stormy as the weather outside. Suddenly, lightning scribbled a jazzed streak over the San Fernando Valley and there was a rolling clap of thunder. "Don't worry, Walt," one of the animators quipped, glancing heavenward. "We'll get it yet."

My brother Walt is gone, but his influence still lingers like a living presence over the studio where he turned out the cartoons, nature films, and feature movies that made him known and loved around the world. Even now, as I walk around the studio lot, I half expect to encounter that gangly, country-boy figure, head bowed in thought about some new project. Walt was so much the driving force behind all we did, from making movies to building Disneyland, that people constantly mention his name as if he were still alive. Every time we show a new picture, or open a new feature at Disneyland, someone is bound to say, "I wonder how Walt would like it?" And when this happens, I usually realize that it was something he himself had planned. For my imaginative, industrious brother left enough projects in progress to keep the rest of us busy for another twenty years.

Walt was a complex man. To the writers, producers, and animators who worked with him, he was a genius who had an uncanny ability to add an extra fillip of imagination to any story or idea. To the millions of people who watched his TV show, he was a warm, kindly personality, bringing fun and pleasure into their homes. To the bankers who financed us, I'm sure he seemed like a wild man, hell-bent for bankruptcy. To me, he was my amazing kid brother, full of impractical dreams that he made come true.

Recently, his family and mine—wives, children, and grandchildren—went back to our old hometown of Marceline, Missouri, for ceremonies celebrating the issuance of the Walt Disney commemorative stamp. As the gleaming Santa Fe train rolled across the green Midwestern prairie, memories of the pleasant years that Walt and I spent there inevitably flooded back.

The apple orchard and weeping willow stand green and beautiful at our old farm, where Walt sketched his first animals. I recall how Walt and I would snuggle together in bed and hear the haunting whistle of a locomotive passing in the night. Our Uncle Mike was an engineer, and he'd blow his whistle—one long and two shorts—just for us. Walt never lost his love of trains. Years later, an old-fashioned train was one of the first attractions at Disneyland.

As far back as I can remember, Walt was drawing. The first money he ever made was a nickel for a sketch of a neighbor's horse.

He studied cartooning in Chicago, and then started a little animated cartoon company in Kansas City that flopped. I was in Los Angeles when Walt, just twenty-one, decided to try his luck in Hollywood. I met him at the station. He was carrying a cheap suitcase that contained all of his belongings.

We borrowed $500 from an uncle, and Walt started a cartoon series called "Alice in Cartoonland." It was tough going. Walt did all the animation, and I cranked the old-fashioned camera. The Alice cartoons didn't make much of a splash, so Walt started a new series called "Oswald and Rabbit." Oswald did better, but when Walt went to our New York distribution for more money he ran into trouble.

"What kind of deal did you make, kid?" I asked.

"We haven't got a deal," Walt admitted. "The distributor copyrighted Oswald and he's taking over the series himself." Strangely, Walt did not seem downhearted. "We're going to start a new series," he enthused. "It's about a mouse. And this time, we'll own the mouse."

The rest is history. Mickey was the first successful product of Walt's matchless imagination and ability to make his dreams become reality. It was an ability he could turn on for any occasion, large or small. Once when my son Roy Edward had the measles, Walt came and told him the story of Pinocchio, which he was making at the time. When Walt told a story, it was a virtuoso performance. His eyes riveted his listener, his mustache twitched expressively, his eyebrows rose and fell, and his hands moved with the grace of a musical conductor. Young Roy was so wide-eyed at Walt's graphic telling of the fairy tale that he forgot all about his measles. Later, when he saw the finished picture, he was strangely disappointed. "It didn't seem as exciting as when Uncle Walt told it," he said.

Like many people who work to create humor, Walt took it very seriously. He would often sit glumly through the funniest cartoon, concentrating on some way to improve it. Walt valued the opinions of those working with him, but the final judgment was always unquestionably his. Once, after viewing a new cartoon with evident displeasure, Walt called for comments from a group of our people. One after another they spoke up, all echoing Walt's criticism. "I can get rubber stamps that say, 'Yes, Walt,'" he snapped. Then he wheeled about and asked the projectionist what he thought. The man sensed that dissent was in order. "I think you're all wrong," he declared. Walt just grinned. "You just stick to your projector," he suggested.

Bankers, bookkeepers, and lawyers frequently tried to put the brakes on his free-wheeling imagination and were the bane of Walt's existence. As his business manager, I was no exception. "When I see you happy, that's when I get nervous," he used to say. Since Walt would spare no expense to make his pictures better, we used to have our battles. But he was always quick to shake hands and make up.

Walt thrived on adversity, which is fortunate because we had it in spades. Even with Mickey a hit, we were constantly in hock to the banks. When he made his first real financial bonanza with *Snow White,* he could scarcely believe it.

Sure enough, the good fortune was too good to last. *Snow White* made several million dollars when it came out. But Walt soon spent that and then some by plunging into a series of full-length cartoon features and building our present studio.

To keep the studio afloat we sold stock to the public—and it sank immediately from $25 a share to $3. Troubles piled up. The studio was hit by a strike. Then World War II cut off our European market. More than once I would have given up had it not been for Walt's ornery faith that we would eventually succeed.

He drove himself harder than anyone else at the studio. His two daughters, Diane and Sharon, learned to ride bikes on the deserted studio lot on weekends—while Walt worked.

Walt involved himself in everything. During one story conference on the *Mickey Mouse Club* TV show, the story man, pointer in hand, was outlining a sequence called "How to Ride a Bicycle." "Now, when you get on your bicycle . . ." he began. Walt stopped him. "Change *your* bicycle to *a* bicycle," he said. "Remember, every kid isn't fortunate enough to have a bike of his own."

Very little escaped Walt's perceptive eye. Animators often found their crumpled drawings retrieved from the wastebasket with a notation from Walt: "Let's not throw away the good stuff." And that, I think, was his greatest genius: he knew instinctively what "good stuff" was. After others had worked on a story plot for months, Walt would often come in, juggle things around a bit, add a gag or two—and suddenly the whole thing came to life.

Walt demanded a lot of people, but he gave a lot, too. When the Depression hit, and it looked as though we might have to close the studio, Walt gave everyone a raise. Some thought he was crazy, but it gave morale a big boost. He hated to fire anyone, and if someone didn't work out in one job, Walt would try to find a niche where he was better suited. Once, when we were faced with having to drop some animators, Walt found places for them at Disney Enterprises in nearby Glendale, where he was secretly developing plans for what eventually became Disneyland.

The story of Disneyland, perhaps, better than anything else, illustrates Walt's vision and his stubborn determination to realize an idea he believed in. For years, Walt had quietly nursed the dream of a new kind of amusement park. It would be a potpourri of all the ideas conjured up by his fertile imagination. But the idea of sinking millions of dollars into an amusement park seemed so preposterous that he wouldn't mention it to anyone. He just quietly began planning.

As usual, though, he infused all of us with his own enthusiasm when he finally told us about the project. Predictably, we had trouble raising money, but Disneyland did open in July 1955. Since that first day, millions of people, including eight kings and eight presidents, have flocked to see the unique creation of Walt's imagination. Like a kid with a new toy—the biggest, shiniest toy in the world—Walt used to wander through the park, gawking as happily as any tourist.

The overwhelming success of Walt's "crazy idea" triggered a dramatic about-face in the Disney fortunes. Yet success never changed Walt. He remained the simplest of men. He hated parties, and his idea of a night out was a hamburger and chili at some little restaurant. His only extravagance was a miniature railroad that ran around the grounds of his home.

"What do you do with all your money?" a friend once asked him. Pointing to the studio, Walt said, "I fertilize that field with it." And it's true that Walt plowed money back into the company almost as fast as it came in. When Disneyland opened, it had twenty-two attractions and cost $17 million. Today it has fifty-two attractions and the total investment is $100 million.

Typical is what happened one day when Walt and Admiral Joe Fowler, Disneyland construction supervisor, were looking over the parks' Rivers of America attraction. It was the scene of feverish activity. The paddle-wheeler *Mark Twain* was puffing around a bend. Two rafts crowded with children were crossing to Tom Sawyer's island. Several canoes, manned by real Indians, were racing. It looked as though the whole flotilla was about to converge in one huge collision.

"Gosh, isn't that great!" Walt exclaimed. "Do you know what we need now?

"Yeah," grunted Fowler. "A port director."

"No," Walt said. "Another big boat!" And he got one, the *Colum-*

bia, a full-scale replica of the first American square-rigger to sail around the globe.

Being solvent for the first time since he started in business gave Walt a chance to develop other ideas. These included the development of Mineral King (an Alpine-like valley high in the Sierra Mountains), a California Institute of Art, for which he donated the land and several million dollars, and, most ambitious of all, a $100-million Disney World and City of Tomorrow in Florida.

Tragically, in the midst of all this activity, Walt was stricken with his fatal illness. I heard him refer to this cruel blow only once. "Whatever it is I've got," he told me, "don't get it."

I visited him in the hospital the night before he died. Although desperately ill, he was as full of plans for the future as he had been all his life.

Walt used to say that Disneyland would never be finished, and it never will. I like to think, too, that Walt Disney's influence will never be finished; that through his creations, future generations will continue to celebrate what he once described as "that precious, ageless something in every human being which makes us play with children's toys and laugh at silly things and sing in the bathtub and dream."

1901 Born in Chicago, Ill.—the fourth of five children.

1917 Leaves school at 16 to become a volunteer ambulance driver during WWI. Decorates the sides of his ambulance with cartoons.

1922 Moves to Hollywood with hopes of directing. Walt and brother Roy set up shop in their uncle's garage—Walt animates, Roy is cameraman. The following year, the first Disney cartoon, *Alice in Cartoonland,* reaches theaters.

A Wonderful Life

1925 Proposes to Lillian Bounds. Two daughters follow—one by adoption.

1928 On a train ride, Walt doodles a mouse with white gloves. *Steamboat Willie* opens to raves in NYC, and Mickey goes on to becomes a worldwide phenomenon: Topolino in Italy, Miki Kuchi in Japan, Michel Souris in France, El Raton Miguelito in Latin America, and Mikki Maus in Russia. Disney: "I've tried to figure out why Mickey appealed to the whole world. Everybody's tried to figure it out. So far as I know, nobody has. He's a pretty nice fellow who never does anybody any harm, who gets into scrapes through no fault of his own, but always manages to come out grinning."

1937 *Snow White and the Seven Dwarfs* grosses $8 million and wins an Oscar. But the following year, with outsized ambitions for Mickey, Walt produces *Fantasia* for a then staggering $2.3 million. Profits fall short of expectations. Disney is forced to go public.

1942 During WWII, the U.S. Army takes over most of Disney's studio to produce home-front propaganda—sandwiching *Der Fuehrer's Face* between *Dumbo* and a reissue of *Snow White*.

1947 A dark year: Disney testifies before the House Un-American Activities Committee and names several employees. Historians later ascribe this to an animosity toward labor unions.

1950 *Cinderella* debuts to huge success.

1953 Despite investor skepticism, Walt presses forward with plans for a theme park. When Disneyland opens two years later, a counterfeiter floats fake tickets and 30,000 people enter the park. Rides break. Stands run out of food and drinks. But Walt presses forward, fixes problems, and the park receives 1 million visitors in the first seven weeks—an unqualified success. On his creation: "Disneyland will never be completed. It will continue to grow as long as there is imagination left in the world." And: "I hope we don't lose sight of one thing—that it was all started by a mouse."

1958 Settles on Orlando, Fla., for second Disneyland, purchasing 27,000 acres for $5 million.

1964 Releases the most successful of his nonanimated movies, *Mary Poppins,* and receives the Medal of Freedom from President Johnson.

1966 By now his movie studio is turning out six new films and several television shows, and his second park is almost ready. But Disney is diagnosed with lung cancer and dies, age 65—having founded an empire on a mouse, transformed it into a $100 million/year entertainment company, and picked up 29 Oscars, four Emmys, and more than 700 awards along the way.

LENNY BRUCE

By Rev. Howard Moody, friend

L enny Bruce's death was no more untimely or uncalled for than the attacks upon his life and livelihood by an indignant society. He tore the skin off every phony reaction in this human existence of ours.

It would be more honest and faithful if we remembered him for those traits and characteristics that ministers and rabbis usually omit from their memorial services. There are three characteristics of his that I especially want to recall: his destructiveness, his unbearable moralism, and his unstinting pigheadedness.

First, his destructiveness: he was a comic who demolished our cultural icons with relentless precision. There was no taboo so forbidding, no shibboleth so sacred, that it could not be exposed and cut out by his probing, surgical humor. Like a shaman, he exorcised and destroyed the demons that plagued the body of a sick society. He exposed mercilessly the ersatz ethics and hollow religiosity of all of us, and he punctured every piece of pomposity and self-righteousness. He was truly a destroyer—of sham, hypocrisy, prejudice, and all true violations of human dignity.

Second, his unbearable moralism. To the public who saw only the Bruce who was a mutation of the mass media—a man obsessed with "dirty words" and a breaker of the law—they would never understand that behind the frantic and tragic showbiz life he was a true moralist. Even his dirty-word "monologues" were a part of a crusade in semantics in which he sought to clean up the so-called "obscenities" and make them represent the beautiful things of human life, part of the joys of life that taboos and mores had made dirty and unmentionable. Back of all the humor and comedy was the evangelical preacher lashing out in honest rage at all the moral deceptions of a terribly immoral society. He backed religion up against the wall of its presuppositions and whipped it with the lash of its own confessions. No institution or individual was spared the sting of his abrasive and moralizing humor.

Finally, his pigheadedness: he was a man possessed of an innate stubbornness that refused to buckle under when his comedy became controversy. He wouldn't believe that what he said was really "obscene" and "dirty," and he endured one of the vilest and most vicious campaigns of personal harassment and persecution ever perpetuated by the law-enforcement officials, not against his personal morality—in that, he was no better or worse than most of us—but against what he was saying in his acts. Finally, he was blackballed in most nightclubs in this country, but he never compromised what he was doing. There is no evidence that he ever sold out to anyone or anything but perhaps his own discouragement and despair.

Of all the things that we might remember about Lenny Bruce,

this ought to stand out—that he offended and exposed every one of us in his devastating attack upon the moral conscience of America.

May God console those who loved and were loved by Lenny Bruce, may God forgive all those who participated and acquiesced in the deprivation of his livelihood while he lived, and may God grant all of us the "shalom" that comes from laughing at ourselves.

1925 Born Leonard Alfred Schneider in Mineola, N.Y.

1930 His parents divorce, and Lenny goes to live with relatives.

1946 Discharged from the navy, Lenny studies acting under the G.I. Bill—getting his first big break on *Arthur Godfrey's Talent Scouts*. The next few years are spent on the comedy-club circuit. Eschewing "a rabbi, a Polack, and a Greek walk into a bar," Bruce sprinkles his act with four-letter words and pungent social satire, stripping away the banality of every-day life.

1947 Changes his name to Lenny Bruce.

1949 Marries Honey Harlow, a striptease "dancer with alabaster breasts."

1951 Arrested for impersonating a panhandling priest as he solicits "dona-tions" for a leper colony run by the Brother Mathias Foundation in British Guiana. Bruce's penchant for material with a high shock value lands him in constant trouble with the law—confirming opinions that he is either a radically relevant social satirist, or just "obscene." Although he does his utmost to antagonize audiences, Bruce shows an air of morality beneath profanity that makes his lapses in taste forgivable—even necessary. Race, religion, motherhood: nothing is sacred.

1957 Divorces Honey.

1961 In his historic performance at Carnegie Hall, Bruce revisits his old stomping grounds: religion, politics, race, abortion, and the Ku Klux Klan. He is later arrested for obscenity, but the jury acquits.

1964 By now a target for the Manhattan D.A., Bruce is arrested after under-cover police witness a Greenwich Village show. (To the police: "I didn't *do* it, man, I only said it.") In a widely publicized six-month trial, he is con-victed—despite support from William Styron, Norman Mailer, and James Baldwin, who proclaim him "a satirist in the tradition of Swift and Twain." Goes broke with legal bills. His obscenity trials will become benchmarks in First Ammendment cases for freedom of expression, and fuel later performances with tirades against the police.

1965 At the request of Hugh Hefner, Bruce pens his autobiography—serialized in *Playboy: How to Talk Dirty and Influence People*.

1966 Blacklisted by nearly every comedy club, Bruce overdoses on morphine in the bathroom of his Hollywood Hills home and dies, age 40—having revolutionized stand-up. In 2003, N.Y. governor George Pataki pardons him for his obscenity conviction, the first posthumous pardon in the state's history.

MILTON BERLE

By Larry Gelbart, longtime friend

DELIVERED AT MEMORIAL SERVICE, APRIL 1, 2002
HILLSIDE MEMORIAL PARK, CULVER CITY, CALIFORNIA

I n so short a time, so dramatic a changing of the guard.

So many gifted people, whose offerings did, in fact, help guard our equilibrium and restore our better spirits, who did so much to grant us a reprieve from the harshness of the sadly predictable unpredictability of life.

In a brief, seismic period, we lost not only Milton. We lost Pat Weaver, the extraordinary visionary, who refined the medium that Milton seems to have spawned single-handedly. We lost the seductive voice and deductive mind of Peggy Lee. We lost the world-class designer Richard Sylbert. And the writer with a world of class, Leonard Gershe. We lost the diminutive-in-all-things-but-his-ability-to-delight Dudley Moore. And, never mind that he was ninety-five, we lost the all-too-soon-late Billy Wilder.

I hear you, Milton. Sorry. I know you work alone.

Why is it we're always sold on the idea that the John Waynes and the Ronald Reagans of the world are somehow the best examples, the real representatives of what is best about this country? Why is it the West is supposed to represent the embodiment of American strength and courage?

To me, Milton—with his eastern cheekiness, and his complete unflappability—was as American as stage mom and apple pie.

It is, of course, entirely too easy to exaggerate at a time like this. These occasions always offer a temptation to lay on the superlatives until they all but form a solid, to give Milton one last dynamite, money review—ask for a few moments of silence (which, to him, would be the most unforgivable of insults), and then send him on his way.

But a few things must be said. Not necessarily of the anecdotal variety. There are enough colorful, improbable stories about Milton's legendary life to keep us for so long, it would hardly pay for some of us here to make the trip home. We needn't go into statistics, either. The triumphs he knew, the records he broke, the precedents he set, the careers he had, the number of media he mastered.

But a few things cannot go unsaid.

All the while harboring the near childish wish that he could be sitting out front to hear them.

To even take credit for them, if it pleased him.

I always understood what was perhaps the most fabled of Milton's foibles. His propensity for—how to put it delicately at this time? For giving other people's material a new home.

Jokes are a comic's oxygen. And Milton simply never, ever stopped inhaling.

With a mind like a magnet — clawing his way up from the bottom of the vaudeville bill — Milton knew that, for comedians, it was a matter of the survival of the wittiest. That was at the beginning. If he hijacked any jokes once he got to the top, he must have considered them as mere tribute that was due him as the king. Whatever he took, whenever he took it, let it also be said that he took no prisoners.

Except for those who came to see him perform.

Milton's aim was never to simply entertain. Milton had to annihilate an audience.

Whether that audience was a roomful, a theater full, or an entire nation full of people, Milton's goal was to grab a crowd by its collective throat, and then proceed to vacuum the laughter out of it. He was shameless, outrageous, and — to his everlasting credit — gloriously unapologetic.

But in a lifetime lived right up to crowd each and every corner of it, whatever the line, whatever the shtick, whatever the trick he employed, Milton never conveyed, never once displayed one iota of anger. Loving what he did — being allowed to do it seemingly endlessly — Milton's only enemy was failure.

Onstage, on camera, just simply on — a stance he first struck while still attached to his end of the umbilical cord — luxuriating in the spotlight that was to follow him for the whole of damn near a century — what Milton was was what an audience got. Or at least, that side of him that he chose to show: The cyclonic, near-demonic, kitchen sink comic, who threw out as many lines as it took to reel us in — who minced until we winced — whose chutzpah was enough to make the brashest member of any group blush.

The Morris Office surely must have collected 11 percent of Milton's earnings. No one who ever watched him perform ever saw him give less than a hundred and ten of himself.

Subtlety and sophistication, he saved for his lyrics. His light touch was reserved for his family, for those lucky enough to be included in his circle of friends.

And to be there—to be *always* there—to cushion his vulnerabilities—those insecurities that all the hard-earned laughter in the world could never allay—there was Lorna. Lorna, who gave Milton, in the winter of his life, a springtime that lasted a decade. Years before, there had been the redoubtable Ruth. His daughter, Vickie. His grandkids. Both sets of them. And the son that he named after his friend, the very same Billy Wilder, in a time that was better for all three of them.

One anecdote. I can't resist.

Milton's first trip to the altar was, of course, with the beautiful Broadway showgirl Joyce Matthews. Milton's first trip to the divorce court was also with the beautiful Broadway showgirl Joyce Matthews. When they decided to take a second trip down the aisle, someone asked Milton whatever prompted him to marry Joyce again.

Milton's answer was: "Because she reminded me so much of my first wife."

Chronically unable to resist tinkering with words, I discovered that one of the anagrams for Milton Berle, and an amazingly appropriate one, is: "I'll Be Mentor."

And that, he surely was.

Each time that Milton performed, it was a Master Class—a demonstration of timing and dedication that proved that as lowly an art form as vaudeville could, in an expert's hands, be elevated into a science. Offstage, there was a surprising courtliness about him, a personal grace completely at odds with his professional garishness. His appreciation of the talents of others demonstrated why he was so in tune with the feelings of an audience. He had an abiding respect for excellence—no matter what side of the footlights he found himself on.

Lastly, there were the countless private acts of generosity and kindness he performed that he'd never dream of trotting out to become part of his public act.

We'll always love you, Milton, Pat and I.

We cherished our friendship.

As American as we are, it's still a thrill being singled out by royalty.

Just one more thank you before you go. One last lesson you've taught us today: It's a whole lot easier saying I love you at the beginning than it is at the end.

1908 Born Mendel Berlinger in a five-story Harlem walk-up.

1914 After he wins a Charlie Chaplin impersonation contest, his aggressive stage mother drags him to Edison's movie studios. He catches Chaplin's eye—who directs him in *Tillie's Punctured Romance,* beginning a spate of bit roles in over 50 silent movies.

1921 Makes his vaudeville debut at the prestigious Palace Theater. Changing his name to Berle, he becomes a headliner known for brash comedy.

1943 A stint in Broadway's *Ziegfeld Follies* establishes Berle as bona fide star.

1946 Adopts a daughter, Virginia.

1948 Every Tuesday at 8 P.M., telecast live from NBC Studios in New York, Berle entertains the nation in *Texaco Star Theater.* Audiences love his sight gags, bad puns, funny way of walking, and outrageous costumes. A reputed joke thief, he frequently rankled other performers. To Groucho Marx: "I've stolen some of my best jokes from you." Groucho: "Then you weren't listening."

1951 Signs a 30-year contract with NBC for $200,000/year. Berle becomes known as "Mr. Television," but younger viewers know him as "Uncle Miltie"—an unofficial member of everyone's family. Groucho on Berle's 30-year TV commitment: "That's not a contract, that's a sentence."

1954 *Texaco Star Theater* is renamed *The Milton Berle Show.*

1960 Having exhausted TV, Berle plays Vegas and returns to Broadway, after a 30-year absence, in *The Goodbye People.*

1978 Wins Special Emmy Lifetime Achievement Award.

1980 Launches two decades of television appearances—trading quips on *The Love Boat, CHiPs, Fame, Fantasy Island, Gimme a Break, Diff'rent Strokes, Murder, She Wrote, Beverly Hills 90210, The Fresh Prince of Bel-Air, The Nanny, Roseanne, Sister, Sister,* and many others. On being a TV self-starter: "If opportunity doesn't knock, build a door."

1984 Plays himself in Woody Allen's *Broadway Danny Rose.*

1989 Publishes his fourth book, *Milton Berle's Private Joke File,* featuring 1,000 of his best jokes collected over 80 years in showbiz.

1998 Suffers a mild stroke.

2002 Dies at his home in Los Angeles, age 93. Berle is buried in Hillside Memorial Cemetery.

TUNESMITHS &
TROUBADOURS

LEONARD BERNSTEIN

By Ned Rorem, fellow composer and close friend

WRITTEN IN COMMEMORATION

During the terrible hours after Leonard Bernstein's death, the press called repeatedly with irrelevant questions: How well did you know him? What made him so American? Did he smoke himself to death? Wasn't he too young to die? What was he really like? None of this seemed to matter since the world had suddenly grown empty—the most crucial musician of our time had vanished. But gradually it became clear that there are no irrelevant questions, and these were as good as any to set off a remembrance.

I was nineteen in early 1943 when we met in his West-Fifty-second-Street flat. Despite his showbiz personality, he had, and forever retained, a biblical look, handsome and nervy as the shepherd David who would soon be kind and psalmodized throughout his days. To me, a Midwest Quaker, his aura was Jewish and quite glamorous, while to him I remained something of a reticent WASP who never quite got the point.

How well did I know him? To "know well" has to do with intensity more than with habit. Everyone in Lenny's vast entourage thought himself to be, at one time or another, the sole love of his life, and I was no exception. The fact that he not only championed my music, but conducted it in a manner coinciding with my very heartbeat, was naturally not unrelated to the love. Years could pass without our meeting, then for weeks we'd be inseparable. During those periods he would play as hard as he worked, with a power of concentration as acute for passion as for Passions.

In Milan, in 1954, when he was preparing *La Sonnambula* for La Scala, I asked him how Callas was to deal with. "Well, she knows what she wants and gets it," he said, "but since she's always right, this wastes no time. She's never temperamental or unkind during rehearsal—she saves that for parties." Lenny was the same: socially exasperating, even cruel with his manipulative narcissism (but only with peers, not with unprotected underlings), generous with his professional sanctioning of what he believed in.

Was he indeed so American? He was the sum of his contradictions. His most significant identity was that of jack-of-all-trades (which the French aptly call *l'homme orchestre*), surely a European trait, while Americans have always been specialists. If he did not want desperately to create a self-perpetuating American art, his own music, even the Broadway scores, was a grab bag of every imaginable foreign influence. Night after smoke-filled night we could sit up arguing the point, for Lenny ached to be taken seriously as a sage. Nothing was ever resolved, of course, not so much because musical philosophy is an impotent pursuit, as because he was less a thinker than a doer. Yes, he was frustrated at forever being "accused" of spreading himself thin, but this very spreading, like the frustration itself, defined his theatrical nature. Had he concentrated on but one of his gifts, that gift would have shriveled.

I last saw Lenny in May, when, with two other people, we went to a dance program, afterward to a restaurant. His role, as always, was to be the life of the party, but repartee fell flat, the concerned pronouncements were incomplete, his breath distressingly short, and he disappeared like a ghost in the midst of the meal. A month later we spoke on the phone, not about health or music, but about the plight of a young Romanian student without a passport. Lenny could simultaneously focus on his navel and on the universe, even in his agony.

Was he too young to die? What is too young? Lenny lead four lives in one, so he was not seventy-two but two hundred and eightyeight. Was he, as so many have meanly claimed, paying for the rough life he led? As he lived many lives, so he died many deaths. Choking may be have been one cause, but so was overwork, and especially sorrow at a world he so longed to change but which remained as philistine and foolish as before. Which may ultimately be the broken-hearted reason any artist dies. Or any person.

So what was he really like? Lenny was like everyone else only more so, but nobody else was like him.

1918 Born in Lawrence, Mass., to a Jewish family from Russia.

1928 Age 10, Leonard eyes a piano, hits the keys and cries, "Ma, I want lessons!"

1940 During his last semester at Harvard, he produces *The Cradle Will Rock*, a left-wing musical banned in Massachusetts. Graduates cum laude. Taking a stint playing piano at the Village Vanguard in NYC, Bernstein is encouraged by Aaron Copland to become a conductor but freely admits he "doesn't know a baton from a tree trunk."

1941 Heads to the Curtis Music Institute to learn the difference.

1943 Opportunity knocks: The director of the N.Y. Philharmonic falls ill and Bernstein is invited to conduct. Encouraged to change his name to improve his chances of success, the young musician replies, "I'll do it as Bernstein or not at all!" The concert is broadcast on radio. A rave appears on Page 1 of the *New York Times*. And the name "Leonard Bernstein" is suddenly known throughout the country.

1944 Debuts *Fancy Free,* a ballet with choreographer Jerome Robbins— establishing both men as geniuses in their fields. Later they collaborate again, in Broadway's *On the Town,* causing many to pronounce Bernstein savior of the American musical at an improbably young age.

1948 Bernstein is a familiar sight at Lindy's, the Russian Tea Room, and other NYC haunts, setting tongues wagging, and females swooning when he takes the podium. Watching him conduct, Tallulah Bankhead announces, "Darling, I have gone mad over your back muscles."

1951 Marries Chilean actress Felicia Montealegre. Three children follow.

1953 First American to conduct at Italy's La Scala opera with soprano Maria Callas. Back home, the left-wing liberal narrowly escapes being blacklisted—going on to support the radical Black Panthers and oppose the Vietnam War in later decades. On politics: "A liberal is a man or a woman or a child who looks forward to a better day, a more tranquil night, and a bright, infinite future."

1957 Retelling Shakespeare's *Romeo and Juliet* in NYC, *West Side Story* becomes Bernstein's most beloved music—revolutionizing and reinvigorating the American musical.

1958 Named conductor and director of the New York Philharmonic—at 40, the youngest director to assume the post. Some find him distracting: Bernstein goes into fits of exultation, often leaving the podium entirely, rising like a rocket in triumphant climax.

1971 Conducts his thousandth performance with the Philharmonic.

1976 Separates from Felicia. Notorious for his promiscuity, Bernstein has had several homosexual relationships. After separating, he lives with partner Tom Cochran but returns to care for Felicia when she becomes terminally ill.

1982 Publishes his fourth book, *Findings*.

1989 On Christmas, conducts the Berlin Celebration Concerts on both sides of the Berlin Wall as it is being demolished. The concert is seen in over 20 countries by 100 million. Reworking *Ode to Joy* with typical flair, Bernstein substitutes the word "freedom" for "joy," claiming, "I'm sure Beethoven would have given us his blessing."

1990 Dies of a heart attack, age 72—one of the most prodigally talented musicians in American history. Having brought a bewildering versatility to the symphony, Broadway, ballet, film, and television, Bernstein offered this explanation of his hydra-headed success: "To achieve great things, two things are needed; a plan, and not quite enough time."

DUSTY SPRINGFIELD

By Neil Tenant, Pet Shop Boys collaborator

DELIVERED AT FUNERAL, MARCH 12, 1999
HENLEY-ON-THAMES, ENGLAND

A photographer I know was asked last week if he could somehow sum up Dusty Springfield—what made her so special? His answer was simple: "Dusty was fab."

When I was growing up in the sixties, Dusty was the very essence of fabness: the hair, the eye makeup, the tender voice. She was always there on the radio and the TV. It gave me a funny feeling hearing her. She was fab. Twenty years later, in the eighties, Chris and I wrote a duet with the songwriter Allee Willis, and decided we wanted Dusty to sing it with us. It seemed to take ages to track her down, but we were prepared to wait. No one else would do.

Believe it or not, at the time people were quite dismissive of the idea. "Her voice isn't what it was," a friend stated. "Jerry Wexler said she was without doubt the most difficult singer he's ever worked with," a journalist told me about the *Dusty in Memphis* sessions. Then we were told that she'd agreed to do it. The record company wasn't keen. Wouldn't someone more up-to-date be better? We stuck to our guns. She probably wouldn't turn up, anyway. Dusty's fortunes and misfortunes in the seventies and early eighties had created a powerful myth, fueled by rare public appearances. You didn't know what to expect.

On the appointed day, she arrived punctually in the studio wearing black leather, very much the mid-eighties diva, clutching the song lyrics heavily underlined and annotated. She was charming and a little shy, chatted about her cats, enthused about all the recording technology—Dusty loved studio technology; she once said to me "I wish I was a machine so I could get the right sound more easily"—and reminisced about having laryngitis throughout the recording of *Dusty in Memphis*, which is why, she said, she sounded the way she did. We were in awe of her. "What do you want me to sound like?" she asked, after we'd played through the backingtrack, and she seemed surprised by the answer: "You." She got behind the microphone and sounded so like her it was incredible. We all smiled at each other in the control room, thrilled to be in the presence of such greatness.

We didn't see her again until several months later, for the video shoot. There one felt in the presence of a star. My recollection is of Dusty out of bounds in her dressing room for hours with two makeup artists and three hairdressers, one of whom fled downstairs shrieking, "It looks like she's had that wig in the washing machine!" When she emerged, tense instructions were issued to the director about what she would and wouldn't do. I think it was her first video. I realized how insecure she sometimes felt, but as the day went on she relaxed and, by the end, was throwing her hands about as though it was 1964 and we were all *Ready! Steady! Go!* together.

The record was a hit everywhere, even America. Dusty was back. "I can feel I'm getting my power back," she said one day while we were recording "Nothing Has Been Proved" for the film *Scandal.* She was amazing to work with in the studio, incredibly intelligent at phrasing and arranging her vocal so that every verse and chorus sounded different from each other, painstakingly building up to a thrilling climax. A complete perfectionist. You could learn so much from her.

She loved music and always knew what was going on. "I really like garage music," she told me one day. "Yeah, it's great," I enthused, but really it was the first time I'd heard of it. It was the same in the sixties. Dusty was a fan of Motown before most British musicians knew anything about it, and pushed in the studio for her big, Phil Spector–meets-Motown sound. In those days, women weren't expected to be involved in the recording process, but Dusty knew what she wanted and how to get it. As a result, her sixties' albums still sound fresh and exciting. In America she had huge respect. *Dusty in Memphis* is a soul classic.

She was quite difficult to get to know and, producing her, I always thought, "Who am I to tell Dusty Springfield what do?" But we loved her and knew that sometimes it could be difficult being Dusty, being an icon. "You make me feel calm," she observed to us, and she was very funny and sweet, a bit nutty. Someone once told her about a pop singer who said he was always so pushed for time that he had all his food liquidized and then drank it. "Oh what a good idea" was Dusty's response.

She gave us a book about Teddy Bears and lived a life dominated by cats. When she moved back to Europe, she lived in Amsterdam because they didn't have quarantine regulations there. Finally she bit the bullet and put her beloved cats in quarantine in Britain so she could move home again. Not long after their release, one of them was run over and killed. The album we worked on was dedicated to him: "To: Malaysia, my late cat . . . May the great litter box in the sky have room for us all."

We didn't see her in the last few years. When she sang on *Later with Jools Holland*, I phoned her up to tell how great she was doing "Where Is a Woman to Go?" with Alison Moyet and Sinead O'Connor. "Sometimes your friends aren't available to pick you up when you're down," she sings in that song. At one time, people might have imagined that Dusty would come to a tragic end, but she proved them wrong and, it seems to me, ended her life as a grande dame with her OBE [Order of the British Empire], her Rock and Roll Hall of Fame induction, the boxed sets, the big house in Henley.

One of the most annoying things about dying is that you don't get to hear what people say about you once you've gone. I think Dusty would have been amazed and moved to learn how much she means to people, what an impact her singing has made, what fondness people feel for her. The British have always taken pop music surprisingly seriously, and they know that Dusty Springfield was unique, a soul singer, a star, the real thing. Dusty's voice is always there to lift you up when you're down. I feel proud that we knew her and worked with her and played a small part of her fabulous life. She was fab, and because of her music, she always will be.

1939 Born Mary Isobel Catherine Bernadette O'Brien in London.

1950 Attending convent schools, Mary discovers Peggy Lee—whose come-hither style is a major influence. Asked by nuns about her career hopes, she brazenly replies, "I want to be a blues singer!"

1959 Singing alongside her brother, she changes her name to Dusty Springfield, and their singles such as "Silver Threads" and "Golden Needles" cross the Atlantic.

1963 Goes solo. The following year, "I Only Want to Be with You" becomes her first hit—launching Dusty onto the club scene in a towering blonde beehive, panda-eye makeup, and a voice of heartbreaking urgency.

1964 Gets deported from South Africa when she refuses to play racially segregated concerts.

1966 Alongside the Beatles and the Rolling Stones, Dusty helps lead the British Invasion. Following her frequent trips to the U.S., she takes the Motown sound back to England and is subsequently dubbed the White Queen of Soul—one of the finest singers to emerge from the froth of the Swinging Sixties. Other singles follow: "Wishin' and Hopin'" (1964), "You Don't Have to Say You Love Me" (1966), "The Look of Love" (1967), and the irrepressible "Son of a Preacher Man" (1969).

1969 Her magnum opus, the *Dusty in Memphis* album, is widely regarded as a pop masterpiece. It barely cracks the *Billboard* charts.

1973 On the heels of several failed albums, her career goes into freefall. Tells *London Evening Standard* that "her affections are as easily swayed by a woman as a man." But in spite of being heralded as a gay icon—replete with glamour and survivalist spirit—she never quite comes out of the closet. Throughout her life, Dusty operates on two levels: a real person and her own brilliant invention. Blonde who is really brunette. The nation's sweetheart who is actually a lesbian. When she musters the courage to tell her parents, she is devastated by their refusal to take her seriously.

1975 Moves to Los Angeles. Her high-partying lifestyle takes its toll, though, and she tries to commit suicide.

1981 Moves to Toronto claiming, "America was very good to me, and very bad to me, and it needed to be both."

1985   Attempts a comeback, unsuccessfully. But two years later, the Pet Shop Boys invite her to duet on "What Have I Done to Deserve This"—spawning a worldwide hit and a new generation of fans. Suddenly, she is golden again. "I'm really grateful to the Pet Shop Boys. They had the faith in me that I didn't have. They saw something in me that I was about to lose."

1995   Recording her last album, *A Very Fine Love,* Dusty is diagnosed with breast cancer. Retreats to her house in the countryside.

1999   Inducted into the Rock and Roll Hall of Fame a year earlier, Dusty dies of breast cancer—six weeks shy of her 60th birthday. She is quoted in the papers as saying that she wanted to die as Mary O'Brien, but her funeral has all the dramatic flourishes of Dusty the Star: Traffic stops. Fans line the streets. And as the coffin leaves the church to the strains of *You* "Don't Have to Say You Love Me," she receives a standing ovation.

JERRY GARCIA

By Robert Hunter, longtime songwriting partner

DELIVERED AT FUNERAL, AUGUST II, 1995
ST. STEPHEN'S CHURCH, MARIN COUNTY, CALIFORNIA

Jerry, my friend,
you've done it again,
even in your silence
the familiar pressure
comes to bear, demanding
I pull words from the air
with only this morning
and part of the afternoon
to compose an ode worthy
of one so particular
about every turn of phrase,
demanding it hit home

in a thousand ways
before making it his own,
and this I can't do alone.
Now that the singer is gone,
where shall I go for the song?

Without your melody and taste
to lend an attitude of grace
a lyric is an orphan thing,
a hive with neither honey's taste
nor power to truly sting.

What choice have I but to dare and
call your muse who thought to rest
out of the thin blue air
that out of the field of shared time,
a line or two might chance to shine—

As ever when we called,
in hope if not in words,
the muse descends.

How should she desert us now?
Scars of battle on her brow,
bedraggled feathers on her wings,
and yet she sings, she sings!

May she bear thee to thy rest,
the ancient bower of flowers
beyond the solitude of days,
the tyranny of hours—
the wreath of shining laurel lie
upon your shaggy head
bestowing power to play the lyre
to legions of the dead.

If some part of that music
is heard in deepest dream,
or on some breeze of Summer
a snatch of golden theme,
we'll know you live inside us
with love that never parts
our good old Jack O'Diamonds
become the King of Hearts.

I feel your silent laughter
at sentiments so bold
that dare to step across the line
to tell what must be told,
so I'll just say I love you,
which I never said before
and let it go at that old friend
the rest you may ignore.

1942 Born Jerome John Garcia in San Francisco—named after composer Jerome Kern.

1948 Loses a finger in a wood-chopping accident.

1957 Inspired by Chuck Berry—enthralled with the new Danelectro he gets for his 15th birthday—Jerry takes up the guitar.

1959 Joins the army. Nine months, two courts-martial, and eight AWOLs later, he is discharged. Meets Robert Hunter (eulogizer) the following year, and they begin performing in various bluegrass bands together.

1966 The Grateful Dead is born. Garcia: "We are in reality a group of misfits, crazy people, who have voluntarily come together to work this stuff out and do the best we can, and try to be as fair as we possibly can with each other. And just struggle through life."

1967 Band releases their self-titled first album, recorded "in a three-night amphetamine frenzy."

1969 Playing Woodstock in the middle of an electrical storm, they go on without a set list—allowing the music to shape-shift in search of what the band calls "the X-factor," a spontaneous stretch of musical synchronicity. From here on out, they never play a song the same way twice.

1971 *Grateful Dead Live* album sells a million copies. "Deadheads" flock to their concerts. Garcia is baffled: "I feel like we've been getting away with something ever since there were more people in the audience than there were on stage."

1973 Arrested for possession of LSD, marijuana, and cocaine, Garcia is put on probation. He zigzags in and out of rehab for the next decade.

1978 The band performs a series of concerts at the Great Pyramid in Egypt.

1985 Ben and Jerry's Ice Cream pays homage with their newest flavor—Cherry Garcia.

1992 Begins marketing his own line of ties. But touring, recording, and tie-designing prove too much, and Garcia collapses from exhaustion. With the combination of junk food, alcohol, drugs, and heavy smoking, Garcia's health is in freefall.

1993 The Grateful Dead is inducted into the Rock and Roll Hall of Fame. Marries third wife Carolyn Koons on Valentine's Day.

1994 Dies, age 53, of heart failure at a rehab center in Forest Knolls, Calif. His mythical status grows golden when: The Dead call it quits; a wake in Golden Gate Park is attended by 25,000 fans; an asteroid is named after him; and his ashes are sprinkled on the Ganges River on April 4—the same day Buddha reached nirvana and escaped the cycle of reincarnation.

CY COLEMAN

By Larry Gelbart, friend and collaborator

DELIVERED AT MEMORIAL SERVICE, JANUARY 10, 2005
THE MAJESTIC THEATER, NEW YORK CITY

In any field of human endeavor, it falls to a select few to set the standard.

It falls to even fewer to become the standard.

By any measure—by literally hundreds and hundreds of his own measures—Cy Coleman was clearly a member of that select few within the few.

It feels awfully inappropriate, using the past tense in talking about Cy. The wrong tense altogether, talking about a man whose life and work were always so in the moment. A man who was often already in the next moment, and the one after that, starting the next song, finishing the last one. Adding chores, instead of pruning them. Cy was a master juggler, pollinating ever more projects when any particular one threatened to be finished.

Inappropriate, too, since so much of what he committed to paper—and to our memories—still hovers. His work still reaching us, still touching us. So much of what he wrote achieving the goal that only the very best of popular music can: Making a song feel as though it had been written especially, exclusively, with only you in mind.

Cy's brilliance lay in his ability to marry his uncommon gift for original composition to feelings common to us all. He gave the gift of life. The gift of a musical identity. To liars and lovers. To rogues and Romeos. Hookers and heroes. Heels in loafers. And loafers in heels.

His songs at once reflected our experiences. Mirrored our follies. Encouraged our fantasies. In the end, those songs are the keepers of his fame.

Looking up in the caves at Lascaux, in France, you see the famous handprints pressed so indelibly on the ceiling overhead, handprints left there countless millennia ago. They are a silent message, and a prayer, put there by people who wanted to say to ages yet unborn: "We were here." What Cy Coleman leaves behind for the ages yet to come is a far more generous message. It says a good deal more than simply: "We were here."

It says that there were some among us, some who had the almost magical ability to give emotion a sound. A sound that was superior to any other known language. We were here, Cy's song-prints will tell then, and that we never stopped reaching for the stars.

Or for the hand of another. That we spent as much time stumbling, as we did getting back up on our feet. And that when tears weren't an option, we laughed. That is Cy's notable contribution to those who'll become the heirs of his inspiration. The treasures that will connect their time to ours, beyond my personal memories, beyond having had the pleasure of being a member of one of his companies.

I share with all of you the certainty that what lies ahead for Cy's music is an eternity of replays, a never-ending, perpetual reprise of his songs right up until the moment this planet cools and shrinks to the size of an eighth note.

1929 Born Seymour Kaufman in New York City.

1933 Discovers an abandoned piano. Annoyed by Seymour's playing, his father nails the piano shut. Seymour pries the keyboard cover off, continues to play—leading to a recital at Carnegie Hall at age eight.

1948 By the time he graduates from New York College of Music, Coleman has turned away from his classical training, changed his name, and is performing in jazz clubs across the city and on television shows. Tries songwriting.

1952 Carolyn Leigh becomes his songwriting partner, complementing his catchy riffs with urbane lyrics. Together they pen classics like "Why Try to Change Me Now" (1952), "Witchcraft" (1957), and "The Best Is Yet to Come" (1959)—prompting Frank Sinatra to not just record the latter, but also inscribe it on his tombstone.

1960 Coleman and Leigh take to Broadway: *Wildcat* opens with Lucille Ball, spawning the hit "Hey, Look Me Over." But after legendary fights, the duo call it quits.

1964 Meets Dorothy Fields at a party. When asked to team up, the veteran lyricist responds, "Thank God somebody asked!" They deliver the hit *Sweet Charity*. Priding himself on writing memorable melodies, Coleman says: "I like to have fun and be witty—but you can't force it. If it doesn't come naturally, you try too hard to be funny, and the audience can tell."

1973 They work together again on *Seesaw*. Fields dies the following year.

1981 Inducted into the Songwriters Hall of Fame.

1990 Acknowledged as his masterpiece and sporting a book by (eulogizer) Larry Gelbart, *City of Angels* debuts on Broadway. It is a huge critical and commercial success—the first Broadway musical with a jazz score. Collects a Tony for Best Score.

1991 Demonstrating a facility for country music, Coleman composes the score for *The Will Rogers Follies*—right up until opening night. "The only place left to put a piano was in the ladies' lounge. We had to write our new material to the accompaniment of flushing toilets."

1997 Marries Shelby Brown. Three years later, she gives birth to a daughter upon whom the 68-year-old Coleman dotes. Offers Broadway a swan song: *The Life,* a gritty look at pimps and prostitutes.

2002 *Portraits in Jazz* bows at the Kennedy Center. Coleman is 73. "Retirement? It won't work for me," he tells the *New York Times*. "I'm lucky to be in a profession where you can keep getting better. When you play the piano as well as I do, and I can say this unabashedly, you don't like people not to be able to hear you."

2004 Dies of a heart ailment, age 75, weeks before a revival of *Sweet Charity* opens. The lights of Broadway theaters dim in recognition. Survived by a wife and daughter, three Emmys and two Grammys, and a host of hummable songs, Coleman once offered the secret of his success: "You know what the trick is? Just keep on writing."

JOHN DENVER

By Tom Crum, close friend and martial arts instructor

WRITTEN IN COMMEMORATION

Whenever I was with J.D. in the wild places—the mountains, the desert, or the ocean—he would transform. I could see the energy and creativity that he drew from Mother Nature. He became a trusting, playful child in her presence. Whenever we were near cliffs, waterfalls, or deep enough water to leap in, that's what we'd do. Except that only his companions would leap—J.D. would dive. It was as if headfirst was his only way of entry into life.

His courage was heroic. He might be in a very intellectual, political scene, a high-state dinner in Beijing, a meeting with a congressman on the Alaskan Wildlands Bill, or with the Presidential Commission on Hunger, and the next thing you know, J.D. would be standing up and sharing his truth. Even if he didn't have all the precise facts or the politically slick delivery, he came across in a more profound way—heart to heart. And, it made a difference.

John didn't have to know you to be your friend. I remember one snowy evening at J.D.'s house—he was finally relaxing after just returning from another exhausting three-month concert marathon. Irritated at the loud knocking on his door, he opened it to discover another fan who had somehow eluded the security gate. He politely began to tell the guy that it was inappropriate to violate a person's space like this when he noticed that the guy's car had a flat tire. "I won't sign an autograph for you. But I would like to help you change your tire," and proceeded to do so.

John would push strangers' cars out of the snow, help people with their heavy luggage at hotels, and they might never know it was *the* John Denver. No matter how tired or sick or reticent he felt, he would still show up at a charity event or a hospital, and give himself totally to the people, somehow knowing that serving others in need was the best way to rejuvenate himself.

It's the little things done when no one is around that reveal the true character of a person. I'd watch John when he had no idea I was observing, going out of his way to pick up litter. He hated litter. He felt we were throwing garbage on our Mother. Even when we were playing golf, he'd go off into the rough and return with a couple of soda cans and candy wrappers. And if the truth were told, he was in the rough a lot—in golf and in life.

After his second divorce, I sometimes kidded John that he didn't need a second home. He had one—the courthouse. John's real home was wherever he was singing for people. That's where he tapped into his highest spirit, his angelic voice penetrating our hearts and minds about the wisdom of nature, the love of life and the living, and the compassion for the pain and joy of simply being human. Yet, once he put the guitar down, John's human struggles would often resurface. A trying childhood, two painful divorces, along with celebrity public exposure of some alcohol-related incidents challenged his self-worth, blanketing his joy and remarkable accomplishments with varying layers of sadness and anger. I always felt that J.D. was more comfortable in the spirit than in the human condition. His guitar and his voice were the bridge to this spiritual essence, providing him with enormous vitality and total commitment to serving life and the living.

The joys of being a father and having a family were an essential part of John's dreams. The struggle between that reality and his career tore at his heart, and he often would be frustrated in finding the balance.

He loved his three children dearly, and when he was with them, his enthusiasm and devotion had no limits. My son, Eri, and John's son, Zak, played on the same squirt hockey team. They were playing in the Colorado State Hockey Championships in a large arena, but basically the only fans there were the parents or siblings of the players, probably less than a hundred people. No matter. John was so excited, he stood up and sang the national anthem a cappella. We won that game. Afterward, we all went to a pizza place to celebrate. J.D. was still so pumped he bought dinner not only for the whole team, but for everybody in the restaurant.

John was a man of action, a superb outdoorsman. His go-for-it attitude occasionally put him in danger. I was with him 100 feet below the surface of the Pacific, playing with a humpback whale, when his oxygen tank failed. On another occasion he swam by me trapped in an avalanche of snow in the Colorado backcountry, paddling with his head above the swirling white chaos until the avalanche came to rest a 100 yards from its initial fracture line. John wasn't afraid of death or of life and I am certain that he was totally present and focused on doing everything possible to right his plane before it plunged into Monterrey Bay on October 12, 1997.

It's strange how you lose a friend like John Denver and at times you find him as close as he ever was. John didn't just give, he was a gift. When I walked with him, somehow I felt like I was jogging. He had a contribution to make to this earth and humanity and he didn't want to be late. And yet, when he picked up his old guitar and his soul poured out, time would stop for all of us who listened. The wind, the forest, the flowing rivers, and the children came together in one clear voice.

John's spirit is free now. He has no need for shoes. No need for time. He lives with the eagles and rides the wind. John's songs echo through the canyons and through our minds, reminding us how right it is to care. He smiles when we pick up litter or assist a fallen friend. He laughs with us when we live joyfully, and whistles when we walk gently on the earth. There is no need to shed tears any longer for the loss of John. He'd rather that we shed them for the ones walking beside us who may be hurting.

We hug John every time we hug someone in need. We laugh with him every time we have fun with children. And, we share in his spirit when we find our purpose and live a life that celebrates it.

1943 Born Henry John Deutschendorf, Jr., in Roswell, N. Mex., on New Year's Eve.

1964 Changes his name to John Denver due to fondness for Rocky Mountains. After studying architecture at Texas Tech, he lights out for western states to make folk music—minus a diploma, and toting an acoustic guitar from his grandmother.

1967 Marries Annie Martell.

1969 Peter, Paul, and Mary record Denver's "Leaving on a Jet Plane."

1971 Denver follows up with his own "Take Me Home, Country Roads," which becomes a million-seller. Followed by "Rocky Mountain High," spawning the titular hit and vaulting him to worldwide fame.

1974 Named Colorado's poet laureate by its governor. By now, Denver is everywhere—America's wholesome, top-selling singer whose songs are suffused with elegant guitar strumming and kinship for the natural world.

1976 Denver purchases 1,000 acres in Colo. for an environmental school. Later helps create the Arctic National Wildlife Refuge in Alaska.

1977 Tries his hand at acting, opposite George Burns in *Oh God*.

1979 Records the first of two TV specials with the googly-eyed Muppets.

1985 An ambitious year: One of the first Western artists to tour Russia, Denver asks Soviet space officials to launch him to the Mir space station. The cash-strapped Soviets reportedly consider his offer of $10 million before turning him down. Speaks before Senate on behalf of artists, describing how his song "Rocky Mountain High" was dropped from radio because it seemed to be about drug use. And visits Africa to witness the suffering caused by starvation. By now, his humanitarian efforts eclipse his popularity as a singer.

1987 Performs at Chernobyl after nuclear disaster.

1988 Having divorced Annie (for whom he penned "Annie's Song") years earlier, Denver marries Cassandra Delaney. The following year, he has his first airplane accident: A biplane he pilots spins around while taxiing, but Denver walks away unharmed.

1992 Tours China. Divorces Cassandra.

1994 Publishes autobiography, *Take Me Home*.

1997 The Federal Aviation Administration refuses Denver an aviation certificate, due to prior DUI arrest. He pilots his own single-seat fiberglass airplane, but while reaching behind to change the fuel tank he relinquishes control of the aircraft. It plunges 500 feet and crashes into the Pacific. Dead at 53, Denver is identified by his fingerprints, and his ashes are spread over the Rocky Mountains of Colorado.

NINA SIMONE

By Ossie Davis, longtime friend

DELIVERED AT MEMORIAL SERVICE
JULY 26, 2003

I f the trumpet gives an uncertain sound, who shall prepare himself for battle?"

God knows, Nina Simone was a trumpet. And God doubly knows the sound she gave was in no way uncertain. When we needed truth, when we needed clarity, when we needed understanding, when we needed perception, when we needed a healing hand and a restful point of view in our long travail in this our native land, we've always been able to depend upon our artists, our singers, those who express our deepest soul. Even in the days of slavery, there must have been that voice coming through in the cotton field that impressed the slave master. And surely, when he wanted to impress the senator, he would send into the quarters and say, "Who was the girl I heard singing the other day in the cotton field?" And somebody would tell him, and he would send for her. "Come tonight to the Big House and sing us some of them songs for the senator." And she would come, this troubadour, and she would sing; and she would sing of her people, of her God, of their deep tribulations, and of their hope and prayer for triumph. And she would lift the spirits of the party. And at the end of it the slave master would be so proud and bragging to the senator of "look what a treasure I have in my cotton patch." Then he would turn to the girl and say, "You've done so good, I'm gonna do something for you. What do you want?" And she would say, "Master, not so much for me, but a little something if you please for my people. We need food; we need rest; we need recognition. If you could see your way to give us some ease—some comfort—to make it just a little bit better?" And the master, still caught up in the triumph of her singing, would say yes. And in that instant, we had found a leader— found somebody to carry our message to power, and somebody who could bring back to the quarters something to serve our needs.

And always, from that day to this, we've been able to depend upon our artists, our singers, our writers to do that same thing. I remember—as I'm sure you do—the sounds of Marian Anderson, and the changes they made in my soul. As I listened to that voice I was transformed. And I might have come into the situation as a nigger, but I was never able to leave her presence as less than a man. And when I heard Paul Robeson—reading and listening and hearing in the simple lyrics all the instructions I needed, all the support that I needed, the message from on high—I was reassured. I was stabilized.

Nina is of and in that same tradition. In the midst of the struggle, when we were doing our very best—hoping that the world and our country would be impressed by our behavior—things so often went the other way. And Nina summed up the situation in a way

213

that was shorter, sweeter, to the point, than even our most eloquent speakers. She looked at the horror and she said, "Mississippi. Goddamn." She needed no other words to describe that situation—the pain and the agony. Oh, she was a great one.

And we have had in our history many great ones like that. And the powers that be, who are not happy with our progress, the powers who want to keep us down, to keep us back, are very well aware of the value of these artists to us. And from time to time whenever the struggle gets hot, they're always trying to pick out the saber, the person who represents our deepest aspiration, and attack them—like they attacked Paul, like they attacked Harry Belafonte. In fact, just a few days ago, they attacked Danny Glover. These are our trumpets; they give us no uncertain sound. We will not let you take them from us. We will not let you demonize them. We will not let you silence their voices. They still provide us leadership and example, and therefore we ourselves will rise—because their voices summon us to rise, the trumpet that they represent calls us to battle. And so on July 31st, right here in this church, we are going to rally, to make a statement to the Powers That Be that "touch not those who have been anointed to represent our deepest spiritual interest." We will not allow you to silence them because we know if you silence them, you silence us. And if you silence us, you silence the people who added—by their blood and by their sweat, and by their death—the spiritual content of the Constitution of this country. You will not touch them.

So, Nina, you may not be there physically when we assemble once again, but your spirit will, your example will. And in our spirit, we'll meet, we'll consult with each other, we'll come up with our strategy and our tactics and we will take the next step because the trumpet that you represent is not uncertain.

And think of the importance, as I cease, of what the trumpet has always meant. In the battle—the heat of battle when nobody knows what's happening, you don't know what's going on—you depended on the trumpet to give you instructions. If the trumpet said "charge," you charged; if it said "move to the left," move to the left; if the trumpet said "retreat," let's get the heck out of here. But always, you depended on the trumpet to tell you the truth. But now, look what has happened a short while ago to the principle, to the trumpet that should speak the truth to the American people. They told us that there was a tyrant who had weapons of mass destruction, set on being able to kill us in very short order, and therefore we had to move right away to eliminate him and his weapons of mass destruction. They told us there was a connection between the Taliban and the terror groups, and this evil man in Iraq; they have found no such connection. What kind of trumpet is that? When that trumpet calls again for war, how will we respond? Nina Simone was not of that ilk. "If the trumpet gives an uncertain sound, who shall prepare himself for battle?" God knows Nina Simone was a trumpet, and God doubly knows the sound she gave us was by no means uncertain.

1933 Born Eunice Waymon, in Tryon, N.C.—one of eight children in a poor family.

1943 Age 10, Eunice sings in church and shows talent as a pianist. But at her debut recital, her parents are forced to move from their front-row seats to make room for whites—embedding the anger of inequality in her.

1950 Leaves Jim Crow South for NYC, where she studies at Juilliard, thanks to black benefactors.

1954 Unable to fulfill her dream of being America's first black concert pianist, she debuts in an Atlantic City bar—changing her name (and tipping her hat to French actress Simone Signoret). When the bar owner demands she add vocals, Simone does, drawing large audiences fascinated by her eclectic repertoire and sly sexuality. She resists categorization: "To most white people, jazz means black, and jazz means dirt, and that's not what I play. I play black classical music."

1957 Gets an agent. Debuts at Carnegie Hall. Writes to parents, "I'm where you always wanted me to be, but I'm not playing Bach."

1959 Becomes famous for "I Loves You Porgy"—her only Top 10 hit in the U.S., but it sells over a million copies.

1960 Heavily immersed in the civil rights movement, Simone unleashes her deep voice in defiance: "Mississippi Goddam" becomes a civil rights anthem—giving expression to an experience that most white Americans could scarcely imagine, and that few black artists dared put into words. More than a protest singer, though, Simone moves effortlessly between genres—covering gospel, folk, jazz, and blues in a single concert, long before record executives come up with the term "crossover."

1971 After disagreements with agents and record labels, Simone leaves America, charging racism. "I like being on stage, but when it comes to show business itself and the pirates who run it, no, I don't like it at all." France welcomes the recalcitrant Simone.

1978 U.S. homecoming: After withholding income tax to protest the Vietnam War, she is arrested for tax evasion when she returns. For the next ten years, Simone moves restlessly around the globe, absorbing African, European, and Caribbean influences before resettling in France.

1992 Her autobiography, *I Put a Spell on You*, hits bookstores, recounting two marriages and a string of relationships with powerful, often violent men.

1995 Shoots her neighbor's son with a BB gun after he disturbs her concentration—sealing her reputation as a volatile personality. But on stage, she relaxes and regales her adoring audiences with humorous anecdotes from her early career. And occasionally insults them. Her regal bearing earns her the title "High Priestess of Soul."

2003 Dies in her sleep, age 70, a quiet finish to a spirited life. Once asked about her impassioned artistry, she said: "There's no other purpose for us except to reflect the times, the situations around us and the things we're able to say through our art, the things that millions of people can't say. I think that's the function of an artist. And of course those of us who are lucky leave a legacy so that when we're dead, we also live on. I hope I will be that lucky."

9/11 HEROES

FATHER MYCHAL JUDGE (FDNY)

By Father Michael Duffy, friend

DELIVERED AT FUNERAL, SEPTEMBER 15, 2001
ST. FRANCIS OF ASSISI CHURCH, NEW YORK CITY

After all that has been written about Father Mychal Judge in the newspapers, after all that has been spoken about him on television, the compliments, the accolades, the great tribute that was given to him last night at the wake service, I stand in front of you and honestly feel that the homilist at Mother Teresa's funeral had it easier than I do.

We Franciscans have very many traditions. You, who know us, know that some are odd, some are good. I don't know what category this one fills.

One of our traditions is that we're all given a sheet of paper. The title on the top says, "On the Occasion of Your Death." Notice, it doesn't say, in case you die. We all know that it's not a matter of if, it's a matter of when. But that sheet of paper lists categories that each one of us is to fill out, where we want our funeral celebrated, what readings we'd like, what music we'd like, where we'd like to be buried.

Mychal Judge filled out, next to the word homilist, my name, Mike Duffy. I didn't know this until Wednesday morning. I was shaken and shocked . . . for one thing, as you know from this gathering, Mychal Judge knew thousands of people. He seemed to know everybody in the world. And if he didn't then, they know him now, I'm sure. Certainly he had friends that were more intellectual than I, certainly more holy than I, people more well known. And so I sat with that thought, why me . . . and I came down to the conclusion that I was simply and solely his friend—and I'm honored to be called that.

I always tell my volunteers in Philadelphia that through life, you're lucky if you have four or five people whom you can truly call a friend. And you can share any thought you have, enjoy their company, be parted and separated, come back together again and pick up right where you left off. They'll forgive your faults and affirm your virtues. Mychal Judge was one of those people for me. And I believe and hope I was for him.

We as a nation have been through a terrible four days and it doesn't look like it's ending. Pope John Paul called Tuesday a dark day in the history of humanity. He said it was a terrible affront to human dignity. In our collective emotions, in our collective consciousness, all went through the same thing on Tuesday morning.

I was driving a van in Philadelphia picking up food for our soup kitchen, when I began to hear the news, one after another after another. You all share that with me. We all felt the same. It was at two o'clock in the afternoon that I came back to the soup kitchen, feeling very heavy with the day's events. At four thirty, I received a call from Father Ron Pecci. We were serving the meal to the homeless.

And he said, "It's happened." I said, "What?" And he said, "Mychal Judge is dead."

At that moment, my already strained emotions did spiritually what the World Trade towers had done physically just hours before. And I felt my whole spirit crumble to the ground and turn into a pile of rubble at the bottom of my heart. I sat down on the stairs to the cellar, with the phone still to my ear, and we cried for fifteen minutes.

Later, in my room, a very holy friar whom I have the privilege to live with gently slipped a piece of paper in front of me and whispered, "This was written thousands of years ago in the midst of a national tragedy. It's a quote from the Book of Lamentations: 'The favors of the Lord are not exhausted. His mercies are not spent. Every morning, they are renewed. Great is his faithfulness. I will always trust in him.'"

I read that quote and I pondered and listened. I thought of other passages in the Gospel that said evil will not triumph, that in the darkest hour when Jesus lay dying on the cross, that suffering led to the resurrection.

I read and thought that the light is better than darkness, hope better than despair. And in thinking of my faith and the faith of Mychal Judge and all he taught me and from scripture, I began to lift up my head and once again see the stars.

And so today I have the courage to stand in front of you and celebrate Mychal's life. For it is his life that speaks, not his death. It is his courage that he showed on Tuesday that speaks, not my fear. And it is his hope and belief in the goodness of all people that speaks, not my despair. And so I am here to talk about my friend.

Because so much has been written about him, I'm sure you know his history. He was a New Yorker through and through. As you know, he was born in Brooklyn. Some of you may not know this, but he was a twin—Dympna is his sister. He was born May 11th, she was born May 13th. Even in birth, Mychal had to have a story. He just did nothing normally, no.

He grew up in Brooklyn playing stickball and riding his bike like all the little kids then. Then he put some shoe polish and rags in a bag, rode his bicycle over here, and in front of the Flatiron building shined shoes for extra money. But very early on in his life, when he was a teenager—and this is a little unusual—because of the faith that his mother and his sisters passed on to him, because of his love for God and Jesus, he thought he would like to be a Franciscan for the rest of his life. And so, as a teenager, he joined the friars. And he never left. He never left because his spirit was truly, purely Franciscan, simple, joyful, life-loving and laughter. He was ordained in 1961 and spent many years as a parish priest in New Jersey, East Rutherford, Rochelle Park, West Milford. Spent some time at Siena College, one year I believe in Boston.

And then he came back to his beloved New York. I came to know him ten years after he was ordained. This is ironic: My thirtieth anniversary of ordination was Tuesday, September 11th. This always was a happy day for me, and I think from now, it's going to be mixed.

My first assignment was wonderful: I was sent to East Rutherford, New Jersey, and Mychal was there doing parochial work. In the seminary, we learned a lot of theory, but you really have to get out with people to know how to deal and how to really minister. So, I arrived there with my eyes wide open, my ears wide open. And my model turned out to be Mychal Judge. He was, without knowing it, my mentor, and I was his pupil. I watched how he dealt with people. He really was a people person. While the rest of us were running around organizing altar boys and choirs and liturgies and decorations, he was in his office listening. His heart was open. His ears were open, and especially he listened to people with problems.

He carried around with him an appointment book. He had appointments to see people four and five weeks in advance. He would come to the rec room at night at eleven thirty, having just finished his last appointment, because when he related to a person, they felt like he was their best friend. When he was talking with you, you were the only person on the face of the earth. And he loved people and that showed and that makes all the difference. You can serve people but unless you love them, it's not really ministry. In fact, a description that St. Bonaventure wrote of St. Francis once, I think is very apt for Michael: St. Bonaventure said that St. Francis had a bent for compassion. Certainly Mychal Judge did.

The other thing about Mychal Judge is he loved to be where the action was. If he heard a fire engine or a police car, any news, he'd be off. He loved to be where there was a crisis, so he could insert God in what was going on. That was his way of doing things.

I remember once I came back to the friary and the secretary told me, "There's a hostage situation in Carlstadt and Mychal Judge is up there." I got in the car and drove there: a man on the second floor with a gun pointed to his wife's head and the baby in her arms. He threatened to kill her. There were several people around, lights, policemen, and a fire truck. And where was Mychal Judge? Up on the ladder in his habit, on the top of the ladder, talking to the man through the window of the second floor. I nearly died because in one hand he had his habit out like this, because he didn't want to trip.

So, he was hanging on the ladder with one hand. He wasn't very dexterous, anyway. His head was bobbing like, "Well, you know, John, maybe we can work this out. This really isn't the way to do it. Why don't you come downstairs, and we'll have a cup of coffee and talk this thing over?"

I thought, "He's going to fall off the ladder. There's going to be gunplay." Not one ounce of fear did he show. He was telling him, "You know, you're a good man, John. You don't need to do this." I don't know what happened, but he put the gun down and the wife and the baby's lives were saved. Of course, there were cameras there. Wherever there was a photographer within a mile, you could be sure the lens was pointed at Mychal Judge. In fact, we used to accuse him of paying the *Bergen Record*'s reporter to follow him around.

Another aspect, a lesson that I learned from him, his way of life, is his simplicity. He lived simply. He didn't have many clothes. They were always pressed, of course, and clean, but he didn't have much. No clutter in his very simple room.

He would say to me once in a while, "Michael Duffy"—he always called me by my full name—"Michael Duffy, you know what I need?" And I would get excited because it was hard to buy him a present.

I said, "No, what?"

"You know what I really need?"

"No, what Mike?"

"Absolutely nothing. I don't need a thing in the world. I am the happiest man on the face of the earth." And then he would go on for ten minutes, telling me how blessed he felt. "I have beautiful sisters. I have nieces and nephews. I have my health. I'm a Franciscan priest. I love my work. I love my ministry." And he would go on, and always conclude by looking up to heaven and saying, "Why am I so blessed? I don't deserve it. Why am I so blessed?" But that's how he felt all his life.

Another characteristic of Mychal Judge, he loved to bless people, and I mean physically. Even if they didn't ask. A little old lady would come up to him and he'd talk to them, you know, as if they were the only person on the face of the earth. Then, he'd say, "Let me give you a blessing." He put out his big, thick Irish hands and pressed her head till I'd think the poor woman would be crushed, and he'd look up to heaven and he'd ask God to bless her, give her health and give her peace and so forth. A young couple would come up to him and say, "We just found out we're going to have a baby." "Oh, that's wonderful! That's great!" He'd put his hand on the woman's stomach, and call to God to bless the unborn child. When I used to take teenagers on bus trips, he'd jump in the bus, lead the teenagers in prayer, and then bless them all for a safe and a happy time. If a husband and wife were in crisis, he would go up to them, take both their hands at the same time, and put them right next to his and whisper a blessing that the crisis would be over.

He loved to bring Christ to people. He was the bridge between people and God and he loved to do that. And many times over the past few days, several people have come up and said, Father Mychal did my wedding, Father Mychal baptized my child. Father Mychal came to us when we were in crisis. There are so many things that Father Mychal Judge did for people. I think there's not one registry in a rectory in this diocese that doesn't have his name in it for something, a baptism, a marriage or whatever.

But what you may not know, it really was a two-way street. You people think he did so much for you. But you didn't see it from our side, we that lived with him. He would come home and be energized and nourished and thrilled and be full of life because of you.

He would come back and say to me, for instance, "I met this young man today. He's such a good person. He has more faith in his little finger than I do in my own body. Oh, he's such good people. Oh, they're so great." Or, "I baptized a baby today." And just to see the new life, he'd be enthused. I want just to let you know, and I think he'd want me to let you know, how much you did for him. You made his life happy. You made him the kind of person that he was for all of us.

It reminds me of that very well-known Picasso sketch of two hands holding a bouquet of flowers. You know the one I mean — there's a small bouquet, it's colorful and a hand coming from the left side and a hand coming from the right side. Both are holding the bouquet. The artist was clever enough to draw the hands in the exact same angle. You don't know who's receiving and who is giving. And it was the same way with Mychal. You should know how much you gave to him, and it was that love that he had for people, and that way of relating to him, that led him back to New York City and to become part of the fire department.

He loved his fire department and all the men in it. He'd call me late at night and tell me all the experiences that he had with them, how wonderful they were, how good they were. It was never so obvious that he loved a group of people so much as his New York firefighters. And that's the way he was when he died.

On Tuesday, one of our friars, Brian Carroll, was walking down Sixth Avenue and actually saw the airplane go overhead at a low altitude. And then a little further, he saw smoke coming from one of the trade towers. He ran into the friary. He ran into Mychal Judge's room and he says, "Mychal, I think they're going to need you. I think the World Trade Tower is on fire." Mychal was in his habit. So, he jumped up, took off his habit, got his uniform on, and I have to say this, in case you really think he's perfect, he did take time to comb and spray his hair.

But just for a second, I'm sure. He ran down the stairs and he got in his car and with some firemen, he went to the World Trade towers. While he was down there, one of the first people he met was the mayor, Mayor Giuliani. Later, the mayor recounted how he put his hand on Mychal's shoulder and said, "Mychal, please pray for us." And Mychal turned and with that big Irish smile said, "I always do."

And then kept on running with the firefighters into the building. While he was ministering to dying firemen, administering the Sacrament of the Sick and Last Rites, Mychal Judge died. The firemen scooped him up to get him out of the rubble and carried him out of the building and wouldn't you know it? There was a photographer there. That picture appeared in the *New York Times,* the *New York Daily News* and *USA Today* on Wednesday, and someone told me last night that *People* magazine has that same picture in it. I bet he planned it that way.

When you step back and see how my friend Mychal died, when we finish grieving, when all this is over and we can put things in perspective, look how that man died. He was right where the action was, where he always wanted to be. He was praying, because in the ritual for anointing, we're always saying, Jesus come, Jesus forgive, Jesus save. He was talking to God, and he was helping someone. Can you honestly think of a better way to die? I think it was beautiful.

The firemen took his body and because they respected and loved him so much, they didn't want to leave it in the street. They quickly carried it into a church and not just left it in the vestibule, they went up the center aisle. They put the body in front of the altar. They covered it with a sheet. And on the sheet, they placed his stole and his fire badge. And then they knelt down and they thanked God. And then they rushed back to continue their work.

And so, in my mind, I picture Mychal Judge's body in that church, realizing that the firefighters brought him back to the Father in the Father's house. And the words that come to me, "I am the Good Shepherd, and the Good Shepherd lays down his life for the sheep. Greater love than this no man hath than to lay down his life for his friends. And I call you my friends."

So I make this statement to you this morning that Mychal Judge has always been my friend. And now he is also my hero.

Mychal Judge's body was the first one released from Ground Zero. His death certificate has the number one on the top. I meditated on that fact: Of the thousands of people that we are going to find out who perished in that terrible holocaust, why was Mychal Judge number one? And I think I know the reason. Mychal's goal and purpose in life at that time was to bring the firemen to the point of death, so they would be ready to meet their maker. There are between two and three hundred firemen buried there, the commissioner told us last night.

Mychal Judge could not have ministered to them all. It was physically impossible in this life, but not in the next. And I think that if he were given his choice, he would prefer to have happened what actually happened. He passed through the other side of life, and now he can continue doing what he wanted to do with all his heart. And the next few weeks, we're going to have names added, name after name of people, who are being brought out of that rubble. And Mychal Judge is going to be on the other side of death to greet them instead of sending them there. And he's going to greet them with that big Irish smile. He's going to take them by the arm and the hand and say, "Welcome, I want to take you to my Father." And so, he can continue doing in death what he couldn't do in life.

And so, this morning we come to bury Mike Judge's body but not his spirit. We come to bury his mind but not his dreams. We come to bury his voice but not his message. We come to bury his hands but not his good works. We come to bury his heart but not his love.

Never his love.

We his family, friends, and those who loved him should return the favor that he so often did to us. We have felt his big hands at a blessing. Right now, it would be so appropriate if we called on what the liturgy tells us we are, a royal priesthood and a holy nation. And we give Mychal a blessing as he returns to the Father.

So, please stand. And raise your right hand and extend it toward my friend Mychal and repeat after me. Mychal, may the Lord bless you. May the angels lead you to your Savior. You are a sign of his presence to us. May the Lord now embrace you and hold you in his love forever. Rest in peace. Amen.

CAPT. ROBERT DOLAN (USN)

By Mark Wallinger, best friend

DELIVERED AT MEMORIAL SERVICE, OCTOBER 12, 2001

U.S. NAVAL ACADEMY, ANNAPOLIS, MARYLAND

I can't help looking over this sea of sad faces and thinking Bob is looking down and saying, "Oh sure—have a get-together on the one day you know I can't be there!"

We are really joined here today as two parts of Bob's family: his military family and his loved ones. Since we will never be together like this again, I'd like to share some of Bob's letters.

A few years ago, I got a note from Bob, who was in Newport, Rhode Island, studying at Destroyer School to take over the U.S.S. *John Hancock*. He was up there solo and wanted some company. Bob didn't ask easily, so when he asked, you went.

We were in downtown Newport walking past the building that

served as the Naval Academy during the Civil War. We talked about Joshua Chamberlain, who commanded the 20th Maine at Gettysburg. For those who don't know: Joshua Chamberlain knew if his line crumbled, the battle would be lost—and possibly the Union as well. Out of ammunition, his troops exhausted and outnumbered, he had them fix bayonets. They did.

And on his order he had them charge down the hill, yelling at the top of their lungs. They did. It worked, and the Southern troops scattered and the 20th Maine held the line and the North won at Gettysburg. I asked Bob: How do you get smart people to follow impossible orders like that? Charge down a hill without ammunition into an oncoming and armed enemy that outnumbers you?

Bob said: When you are in those situations, you don't do it for God, or country, or a cause. You do it for the person next to you.

I tell this story in this most sacred of military places, because I know that you in the military understand. But for those of us who were his loved ones, understand that Bob was the guy next to us . . . for our whole lives.

The Captain Dolan you served with was a better friend than he was a Captain. And a better brother to Dan and Chris Dolan than he was a friend. And a better son to Mr. and Mrs. Dolan than he was a brother.

That's how I'll remember Bob Dolan. And I'll know that his spirit—the spirit of a warrior, poet, hero, friend—makes me better for the experience, no matter how much I grieve the loss. I knew him for thirty-five years. It is one of the greatest gifts God has given me. Honored to know him doesn't begin to describe it.

I say warrior, poet, hero, friend, because he was all that. He could quote Shakespeare and Steinbeck and Springsteen in the same breath; was the best-read man I knew; had the soul of a farmer; enough heart for two men; and enough common sense for all of us.

I never saw him mad, never heard him be petty, or unkind. He had a sense of fairness that could only be described as all-American.

I met Bob in first grade at Holy Family in Florham Park, New Jersey. People tell me it's unusual to know friends from grade school, but there are no fewer than seven of us in the chapel today who were there that day in September 1965. That's what kind of friends Bob had. Because that's what kind of friend he was.

When my father died, and we were not as close as we would have liked, I thought of him every day for at least a year. When my mother died after a long illness, I thought of her more than that. Since September 11, I have been unable to get Bob out of my thoughts, which I know from my experiences is natural. I'm told he was the last one found at the Pentagon—following a Captain's code to the end that he be the last one to leave. And today? He is there on my shoulder as I go through my day. I feel his presence here today. I know some of you do, too.

To his daughter, Rebecca, and his son, Beau . . . know that he can see you. He'll watch you grow and make friends and fall in love and live your lives. Embrace his angel on your shoulder, because life can be lonely, the world sometimes cruel and unfair. But he's there going through it with you, still connected. He'll see you make mistakes, too, but that is part of life. Don't sweat it, he would say. He once wrote me and said:

Success is a dynamic concept, not a static one. Don't get caught up trying to pin it down to a moment.

Rebecca, I am the father of three girls, but I never knew a father who talked more about his daughter. September 3, 1988, he wrote: "I miss my family terribly. I won't even begin to describe the joys of a daughter, because . . . my poor ability with words could never do it justice. I miss her, so."

From another deployment . . . "As I'm sure you've noticed, I'm kind of partial to Rebecca. She puts a whole new twist on the deployment thing. When I left Lisa, I knew I was coming home to same person I left. When I leave Becca, even for a couple of weeks, it's like coming home to a whole new person. It's tough."

Rebecca, you are confident and smart and beautiful, much like your father was at fifteen. When the world treats you a little less kind than you'd like, remember it treated him that way at times, too. But he never let it turn his heart cold, or bitter. He rarely complained, and always said that life's difficult lessons were just that . . . lessons.

Beau, you were on his mind as well.

From a letter dated 1993 . . . "Your children are truly the only things on earth that accept you for what you are. Their daddy."

He ended that letter with a quote from Teddy Roosevelt, which he called "my favorite quote of all time and one I try to live by":

> Far better it is to dare mightily things to win glorious
>   triumphs,
> Even though checked by failure,
> Than to take rank with the poor spirits who
> Neither enjoy much . . . nor suffer much
> Because they live in that gray twilight that knows no victory,
>   or defeat.

Beau, these are your father's guidelines for manhood. They are a gift to you. I know. I understood him. I grew up with him. We were altar boys together when we were your age. Played ball and rode bikes forever. And in all his travels and all his experiences, these are the words he tried to live by. Learn them. Embrace them. We'll help you as you go. For you are the son of a hero . . . and you will find that you have many friends you never knew. I know you'll be a good friend in return, because you are your father's son.

Lisa, you were the love of his life. Above all of us, you knew the man he was. He didn't get to say goodbye, I know, but if he could have it would have been poetic. I can only think of a famous letter written by Sullivan Ballou, a major in the Second Rhode Island volunteers, in July 14, 1861, to his wife Sarah . . .

Dear Sarah:

. . . lest I should not be able to write you again I feel impelled to write a few lines that may fall under your eye when I am no more.

I have no misgivings about, or lack of confidence in the cause in which I am engaged, and my courage does not halt or falter. I know how American Civilization now leans upon the triumph of the government and how great a debt we owe to those who went before us through the blood and suffering of the Revolution. And I am willing—perfectly willing—to lay down all my joys in this life, to help maintain this government, and to pay that debt.

Sarah, my love for you is deathless; and yet my love of Country comes over me like a strong wind and bears me irresistibly with all those chains to the battlefield. The memory of all the blissful moments I have enjoyed with you come crowding over me, and I feel most deeply grateful to God and you, that I have enjoyed them for so long.

If I do not return, my dear Sarah, never forget how much I loved you, nor that when my last breath escapes me on the battle field, it will whisper your name . . .

But, if the dead can come back to this earth and flit unseen around those they love, I shall always be with you, in the brightest day and in the darkest night . . . always, always. And when the soft breeze fans your cheek, it shall be my breath, or the cool air your throbbing temple, it shall be my spirit passing by.

Sarah do not mourn me dead; think I am gone and wait for me, for we shall meet again . . .

Sullivan Ballou died two weeks later at the Battle of Bull Run, but those words still ring true today.

Finally, I asked in the beginning that those in Bob's military family understand that he was the guy next to us in our lives. I ask now that his loved ones understand the sacrifices that those in the military make on a daily basis.

From a letter dated 5 September 1993:

> It's quite a struggle I find myself in. Duty to country. Duty to family. Duty to myself. I don't know why but I feel like I'm doing something for all three out here. I feel like I'm not just doing for myself, but doing for other people. I don't think I would feel the same if I were designing oil platforms, or sea walls, which is what my degree is in. Yet, somehow I feel disloyal to Lisa and Becca and Beau. I know Lisa understands, and that Becca and Beau will when they are old enough. But I'm torn. Should I know better? Should I be with them because that's what a father and husband does? There are just no easy answers.

After events from September 11, there seems to be even fewer easy answers for those of us left behind. The family of a hero sometimes must share the burdens and struggle after the hero is gone, as the Dolan family now must. Lisa, Rebecca, and Beau, know that there is a sea of people out here willing to help. Rely on us as we did on your father. For he was the guy next to us . . . in our work, and in our lives. And though we mourn his death today, we will be the people next to you so long as we live.

CHIEF PETER GANCI (FDNY)

By Chris Ganci, son

DELIVERED AT FUNERAL, SEPTEMBER 15, 2001
FARMINGDALE, LONG ISLAND

Today we say goodbye and farewell to Pete Ganci. Fireman, father, and most of all a friend to everyone that ever met him. There is so much I could say about my father. In the few minutes I stand before all of you I can never do him justice. If you knew him, then you felt his infectious personality, his unique dynamism, which made you immediately love and respect him. It mattered not whether you were a foreign dignitary or an average guy on the street, my father made everyone feel equally important.

If you didn't already know, my father was a golf fanatic. He played with the same three guys every Saturday, for eight years. The wager was always a dime in the hole. I recall one Saturday morning last year he complained of a stiff back. "Why?" I inquired. He opened his golf bag and revealed to me what must have been the GNP of a small country—all in dimes.

This was the first year I'd been invited to join him. It's a little-known fact that God and my father had an agreement: it never rained on a Pete Ganci golf day. Surprisingly, the first day I played with him, it drizzled. On the second day we were rained out. On the following Monday, he sat me down for an unusual father/son talk, and in typical Pete Ganci fashion he told me that I was still in and he would just have to try harder. Let's just say it hasn't rained on a Saturday since. Take a look outside. It doesn't rain on Pete Ganci.

My father had more talents, more than just controlling the weather, talents which included picking the perfect wife and mother for his children. My mom is the strongest person I have ever met, and I know that together our family will get through this. There are not too many women who would put up with husbands who are married to their job, but she did it for twenty-nine years.

It gives my family some comfort that my father died the way he would have wanted to, with his men. He made a clear choice that fateful Tuesday morning. He chose to see it through. I don't know what quality it is in firemen that tells them to move toward peril when human nature and self-preservation tell the rest of us to do the opposite. Whatever it is, Pete Ganci had it in spades. He was a true fireman to the bitter end. He was the type of leader that would never send a man into a place he wasn't willing to go himself, and during the past two days I have heard countless stories of how my father's courage and leadership saved lives. It gives me solace knowing that his actions might have spared someone else's son from making this speech.

To all the members of the New York City Fire Department, my father's sacrifice and those of all your fallen brethren were not in vain. As we enter a new chapter in our nation's history, the resolve of the American people and their ability to persevere will never be challenged. It is these characteristics that make us truly American, characteristics that weave together the fabric of the FDNY.

And finally, to me, father, I love you, Dad, and am so proud to have been your son.

CAPT. FRANCIS CALLAHAN (FDNY)

By Capt. James Gormley (FDNY), colleague

DELIVERED AT MEMORIAL SERVICE, DECEMBER 10, 2001
LINCOLN CENTER, NEW YORK CITY

Captains and lieutenants of the New York City Fire Department share a special relationship with other officers of similar rank. When we meet for the first time we introduce ourselves to each other, we shake hands, we measure each other's resolve and fortitude. At Operations, our aggressiveness is based on the trust we share in each other.

Firefighters and their officers share a different, but also special relationship. Officers very literally lead firefighters into harm's way. We go first. If things go badly we are required by our oath and tradition to be the last of our command to leave. Accountability for our men is carved into our heart. Responsibility for our men, their wives and children, is in the depth of our soul.

This is why we are here today. Capt. Frank Callahan is the ranking officer killed at the World Trade Center from our firehouse. He leaves last. I cannot say he will be the last to ever leave. We live in a dangerous world, and we put our boots and helmets on every day.

Captains, especially commanding officers of companies in the same quarters, have a unique relationship. We know each other as no one else ever will. We are commanding officers of complementary companies. We cannot work successfully without each other. There are not many of us; you could fit us in one fair-sized room. We are not always friends. There is too much at stake, but our respect, and trust in each other, is unquestioned.

Frank Callahan was more than my friend, and to call him brother would not do our relationship justice. Frank was my comrade. It's harder to be a comrade than a friend. It's different than being a brother.

Friends and brothers forgive your mistakes. They are happy to be with you. You can relax and joke with them. You can take your ease with them—tell them tall tales.

Comrades are different. Comrades forgive nothing. They can't. They need you to be better. They keep you sharp. They take your words literally.

When a friend dies we miss them, we regret words unspoken, we remember the love. When a brother dies we grieve for the future without him. His endless possibilities. If your brother doesn't die of old age you might never accept the parting. When a comrade dies we miss them, we regret words unspoken, we remember the love, we grieve the future without them. We are also proud. Proud to have known a good man, a better man than ourselves. We respect the need for him to leave, to rest.

Some people equate camaraderie with being jovial. It is anything but. Camaraderie is sharing hardship. It is shouts and commands, bruises and cuts. It's a sore back and lungs that burn from exertion.

It's heat on your neck and a pit in your stomach. It's a grimy hand-shake and a hug on wet shoulders when we're safe. It's not being asleep when it's your turn on watch. It is trust, it is respect, it is act-ing honorably.

You hold your comrade up when he can't stand on his own. You breathe for him when his body's forgotten how. It's lifting a man up who loves his wife and children as much as you love your own. Looking them in the eye for the rest of your life and trying to ex-plain, and not being able to. You kiss them for him. It's laying him down gently when his name appears on God's roll call. It's remem-bering his name. I'll never forget his name. He was just what he was called: Frank. You never had to chase your answer. He said it to your face.

It's at the same time being both amazed and proud that you've known men like him. Looking for your reflection in their image. Seeing it. Knowing you're one of them.

There's a song out of Ireland. A line of it says, "Comrade tread lightly, you're near to a hero's grave." If you ever said that to Frank he would have given you the "look" and pushed past you in the hallway.

Frank was light on his feet but he never tread anywhere lightly. When Frank did something it was like a sharp axe biting into soft fresh pine, with a strong, sure stroke. It was done. It was right. It meant something. It was refreshing. It smelled good.

Quite often we discussed history. The successes and failures of political, military, and social leadership. The depth and broadness of Frank's historical knowledge was astounding.

I've been told Frank enjoyed a practical joke. We never joked to-gether. Rarely laughed. We never sought out each other's company on days off. We never went golfing or fishing. We never went for a hike in the Shawangunk Mountains together. We were often hap-pier apart than we ever were together because we shared the night-mares of command.

We shared problems. We shared stress. We shared dark thoughts that are now front-page news. Incredulous at the failures of leadership that have borne fruit. We shared the proposition of a time and place where few would dare to go. He went there because it was his turn. He called his wife, Angie, before he received his orders to respond. He told her what was going on. He told her things didn't look good; he told her he loved her.

Historically it is said, "They rode to the sound of the guns":

Capt. Frank Callahan
Lt. John Ginley
Firefighter 1 Gr. Bruce Gary
Firefighter 1 Gr. James Giberson
Firefighter 1 Gr. Michael Otten
Firefighter 1 Gr. Kevin Bracken
Firefighter 1 Gr. Steve Mercado
Firefighter 1 Gr. Michael Roberts
Firefighter 1 Gr. John Marshall
Firefighter 3 Gr. Vincent Morello
Firefighter 3 Gr. Michael Lynch
Firefighter 6 Gr. Michael D'Auria
Firefighter 2 Gr. Kevin Shea

Kevin, we are joyful that we got you back. Have no guilt. The same goes for the rest of us. I know what you all did, you got your gear on, found a tool, wrote your name or Social Security number in felt-tip pen on your arm or a leg, a crisis tattoo in case you got found.

We went down there knowing things could go badly. We stayed until we were exhausted, got three hours sleep and went back again, and again. That's what comrades do. Only luck and circumstance separate us from them.

It is significant that we are in Lincoln Center for the Performing Arts. The first performance here was *West Side Story*, the story of this neighborhood. This "Act" is part of that story. It is more than we can absorb in one lifetime, so the story must be told until it makes sense.

It is poignant because the arts have helped mankind deal with reality since stories were told round the fire and we drew on cave walls. The arts help us exercise our emotions. We are surrounded by art and overwhelmed by our emotions. From the pictures children have drawn for us, the poetry, songs, and banners, to the concerts, plays, and operas that we have been invited to attend—use the arts to heal your heart. Exercise your emotions. Feel anger, feel hate, feel love and pride. Run the gamut of your emotions until you settle where you belong, as good honorable men, every inch the equal of our comrades, friends, and brothers. That's what they want. That's what your families need. That's what you deserve.

Frank was a trusted leader, a captain. The best commander I've encountered here, or in the military. It was important to him. We both believed captain to be the most important rank in the department. He was forged by his family, his comrades, every officer and firefighter that he ever worked with. He was tempered by his experience.

History, the record of successes and failures of leadership has caused us to be here. Capt. Frank Callahan did not fail in his leadership. He led his command where they were needed, and he's the last of them to leave. If more of the world's leaders were forged as he was, our world would not be in its current state.

Frank Callahan is a star, a reference point. A defined spot on the map of humanity. Guide on him to navigate the darkness. You will not wander, you will not become lost.

ATHLETES

MICKEY MANTLE

By Bob Costas, longtime admirer

DELIVERED AT FUNERAL, AUGUST 15, 1995
LOVERS LANE UNITED METHODIST CHURCH, DALLAS, TEXAS

It occurs to me as we're all sitting here thinking of Mickey, he's probably somewhere getting an earful from Casey Stengel, and no doubt quite confused by now.

One of Mickey's fondest wishes was that he be remembered as a great teammate, to know that the men he played with thought well of him. But it was more than that. Moose and Whitey and Tony and Yogi and Bobby and Hank, what a remarkable team you were. And the stories of the visits you guys made to Mickey's bedside the last few days were heartbreakingly tender. It meant everything to Mickey, as would the presence of so many baseball figures past and present here today.

I was honored to be asked to speak by the Mantle family today.

I am not standing here as a broadcaster. Mel Allen is the eternal voice of the Yankees and that would be his place. And there are others here with a longer and deeper association with Mickey than mine.

But I guess I'm here, not so much to speak for myself as to simply represent the millions of baseball-loving kids who grew up in the fifties and sixties and for whom Mickey Mantle was baseball.

And more than that, he was a presence in our lives—a fragile hero to whom we had an emotional attachment so strong and lasting that it defied logic. Mickey often said he didn't understand it, this enduring connection and affection—for men now in their forties and fifties, otherwise perfectly sensible, who went dry in the mouth and stammered like schoolboys in the presence of Mickey Mantle. Maybe Mick was uncomfortable with it, not just because of his basic shyness, but because he was always too honest to regard himself as some kind of deity.

But that was never really the point. In a very different time than today, the first baseball commissioner, Kenesaw Mountain Landis, said every boy builds a shrine to some baseball hero, and before that shrine, a candle always burns.

For a huge portion of my generation, Mickey Mantle was that baseball hero. And for reasons that no statistics, no dry recitation of facts can possibly capture, he was the most compelling baseball hero of our lifetime. And he was our symbol of baseball at a time when the game meant something to us that perhaps it no longer does. Mickey Mantle had those dual qualities so seldom seen, exuding dynamism and excitement but at the same time touching your heart—flawed, wounded. We knew there was something poignant about Mickey Mantle before we knew what *poignant* meant.

We didn't just root for him, we felt for him.

Long before many of us ever cracked a serious book, we knew something about mythology as we watched Mickey Mantle run out a home run through the lengthening shadows of a late Sunday afternoon at Yankee Stadium.

There was greatness in him, but vulnerability, too.

He was our guy. When he was hot, we felt great. When he slumped or got hurt, we sagged a bit, too. We tried to crease our caps like him; kneel in an imaginary on-deck circle like him; run like him heads down, elbows up.

It's been said that the truth is never pure and rarely simple.

Mickey Mantle was too humble and honest to believe that the whole truth about him could be found on a Wheaties box or a baseball card. But the emotional truths of childhood have a power to transcend objective fact. They stay with us through all the years, withstanding the ambivalence that so often accompanies the experiences of adults.

That's why we can still recall the immediate tingle in that instant of recognition when a Mickey Mantle popped up in a pack of Topps bubblegum cards—a treasure lodged between an Eli Grba and a Pumpsie Green. That's why we smile today, recalling those October afternoons when we'd sneak a transistor radio into school to follow Mickey and the Yankees in the World Series.

Or when I think of Mr. Tomasee, a very wise sixth-grade teacher who understood that the World Series was more important, at least for one day, than any school lesson could be. So he brought his black-and-white TV from home, plugged it in, and let us watch it right there in school through the flicker and the static. It was richer and more compelling than anything I've seen on a high-resolution, big-screen TV.

Of course, the bad part, Bobby Richardson, was that Koufax struck fifteen of you guys out that day.

My phone's been ringing the past few weeks as Mickey fought for his life. I've heard from people I hadn't seen or talked to in years—guys I played stickball with, even some guys who took

Willie's side in those endless Mantle-Mays arguments. They're grown up now. They have their families. They're not even necessarily big baseball fans anymore. But they felt something hearing about Mickey, and they figured I did, too.

In the last year, Mickey Mantle, always so hard on himself, finally came to accept and appreciate that distinction between a role model and a hero. The first he often was not, the second he always will be.

In the end, people got it. And Mickey Mantle got from America something other than misplaced and mindless celebrity worship. He got something far more meaningful. He got love—love for what he had been; love for what he made us feel; love for the humanity and sweetness that was always there mixed in with the flaws and all the pain that wracked his body and his soul.

We wanted to tell him that it was okay, that what he had been was enough. We hoped he felt that Mutt Mantle would have understood and that Merlyn and the boys loved him.

And then in the end, something remarkable happened—the way it does for champions. Mickey Mantle rallied. His heart took over, and he had some innings as fine as any in 1956 or with his buddy, Roger, in 1961. But this time, he did it in the harsh and trying summer of '95. And what he did was stunning. The sheer grace of that ninth inning—the humility, the sense of humor, the total absence of self-pity, the simple eloquence and honesty of his pleas to others to take heed of his mistakes.

All of America watched in admiration. His doctors said he was, in many ways, the most remarkable patient they'd ever seen. His bravery, so stark and real, that even those used to seeing people in dire circumstances were moved by his example.

Because of that example, organ donations are up dramatically all across America. A cautionary tale has been honestly told and perhaps will affect some lives for the better.

And our last memories of Mickey Mantle are as heroic as the first.

None of us, Mickey included, would want to be held to account for every moment of our lives. But how many of us could say that our best moments were as magnificent as his?

This is the cartoon from this morning's *Dallas Morning News.* Maybe some of you saw it. It got torn a little bit on the way from the hotel to here. There's a figure here, St. Peter I take it to be, with his arm around Mickey, that broad back and the number 7. He's holding his book of admissions. He says, "Kid, that was the most courageous ninth inning I've ever seen."

It brings to mind a story Mickey liked to tell on himself and maybe some of you have heard it. He pictured himself at the pearly gates, met by St. Peter who shook his head and said, "Mick, we checked the record. We know some of what went on. Sorry, we can't let you in. But before you go, God wants to know if you'd sign these six dozen baseballs."

Well, there were days when Mickey Mantle was so darn good that we kids would bet that even God would want his autograph. But like the cartoon says, I don't think Mick needed to worry much about the other part.

I just hope God has a place for him where he can run again. Where he can play practical jokes on his teammates and smile that boyish smile, 'cause God knows, no one's perfect. And God knows there's something special about heroes.

So long, Mick. Thanks.

1931 Born in Spavinaw, Okla.—named after baseball player Mickey Cochrane.

1942 Age 11, plays catcher in Pee Wee League.

1946 A kick in the left shin causes chronic bone infection. Facing amputation, he chooses to undergo several operations—but the injury haunts Mickey for the rest of his life.

1949 Signing with the Yankees for $140/month, the country boy with a telegenic grin takes the sport by storm. Playing shortstop, he later replaces Joe DiMaggio in center field. Spends the off-season working as electrician's helper in the mines.

1951 Rollercoaster year: Marries Merlyn Johnson. Purchases a 7-BR house for his parents, but loses his father to Hodgkin's disease. "I guess that's when I started drinking." Undergoes the first of several knee operations—and for the rest of his career, Mantle plays in pain.

1953 Mickey Mantle, Jr., is born, the first of four sons.

1956 Voted MVP the first of three times. Off field, Mantle develops a reputation as a late-night carouser. On field, his Homeric feats endear him to boys and men everywhere, not just hitting the ball, but hammering it, frequently, from both sides of the plate.

1960 Case in point: Hits the longest home run ever—643 feet, clearing the field roof of Tiger Stadium in Detroit. Becomes the highest-paid baseball player, collecting $75,000/year.

1965 Mickey Mantle Day declared at Yankee Stadium.

1967 Begins playing first base. But by now his legs hurt. His knees hurt. And his batting average sinks.

1969 After 2,400 games for the Yankees, No. 7 announces his retirement— but his taste for high living and good liquor accelerates.

1970 Working on a second career, he accepts a coaching job with the Yankees, starts an employment agency with Joe Namath—Mantle Men and Namath Girls—and continues to draw large crowds to autograph shows and his baseball camps.

1974 Inducted into the Baseball Hall of Fame.

1980 Mickey and Merlyn part ways—though neither files for divorce. Later claims in his autobiography that they hadn't married for love, but rather to please his domineering father.

1985 Publishes autobiography, *The Mick.*

1994 Warned by doctors that his next drink might be his last, he commits himself to Betty Ford. Muses, "God gave me a great body to play with, and I didn't take care of it. I blame a lot of it on alcohol." He stays dry, but the damage is done. The following year he develops liver cancer and undergoes a liver transplant.

1995 Dies from liver cancer, age 63, his wife Merlyn at his bedside. The greatest player on baseball's greatest team, a remorseful Mantle had, only days before, held a press conference. "Don't be like me. God gave me a body and the ability to play baseball. I had everything and I just ..." The flawed folk hero is buried at Sparkman-Hillcrest Memorial Park in Dallas.

ARTHUR ASHE

By Governor L. Douglas Wilder, friend

DELIVERED AT MEMORIAL SERVICE, FEBRUARY 10, 1993
THE ARTHUR ASHE CENTER, RICHMOND, VIRGINIA

You know you usually ask the question when someone has passed: "What were you doing at the time?" And usually there's some kaleidoscope occurrence in your mind that makes you recall, "I was doing this or that." It was quite the reverse with me and Arthur.

I have always remembered when I first met him, and that image has always stayed with me: practicing tennis—by himself. And for those who knew him, they know that he was not a lonely man. But that image said so much of him: solitary and proud and determined.

He was never lonely. No man ever treasured friendship and family more than Arthur. And no one has ever been more open to others. He had a quiet soul amid a very busy and noisy life. And he lived in such a way and he carried that grace and dignity with such aplomb that he served as a model for so many people. Not just youngsters, but so many of us.

Oh, I think he would have preferred mightily to have been known as a great tennis player—not as a great black tennis player. I think he would have preferred to have been known as one who was concerned with his fellow man, and he was. His fate touched him with greatness, and he showed that he would never shrink from his responsibility and the life that followed.

I've read on occasions that some had said he expressed resentment and bitterness about his hometown—Richmond, Virginia—though I never heard him express that with me. Oh, we all expressed our resentment against the status quo. He had his reasons why he didn't. And those of you, especially his colleagues in the tennis world, when you came here with him, you saw the accolades, the crowds, the people who adored and adulated him even then. And yet we remember a composed athlete. We saw his composure even when the umpires were wrong. He didn't berate them.

He knew what it meant to have to be better.

He knew that the standards would have to be higher.

He knew that the calls sometimes would be against him when all the world knew they shouldn't have been.

But he said nevertheless, I'll be a champion. And he was. And he used every fiber of his strength on and off the court to right the world's injustices.

Oh, he didn't seek the counsel of what was popular, nor did he concern himself with plaudits or approvals. He made up his mind, kept his own countenance, and practiced the discipline we've all come to know. And he did what he set out to do.

Though wise men at their end know dark is right
because their words had forked no lightning they
Do not go gentle into that good night . . .
Rage, rage against the dying of light.

And he raged against the cards that were dealt in the latter stages
of his life. He determined that he would not let even that deter him
from that indefatigable job that he was chosen by fate to perform.
And that is the spreading of human kindness and loving kindness.

You know it is said there are ten strong things:

That iron is strong, but fire melts it. . . .
That fire is strong, but water puts it out. . . .
That water is strong, but the clouds evaporate it.. . .
That clouds are strong, but the wind blows them away. . . .
That man is strong, but fear is stronger. . . .
That fear is strong, but wine allays it. . . .
That wine is strong, but sleep overcomes it. . . .
That sleep is strong, but death is far stronger. . . .
But loving kindness survives even death.

1943 Born in Richmond, Va.—son of a parks policeman.

1953 The 10-year-old Arthur finds a tennis patron in physician Walter Johnson.

1960 Tired of traveling from segregated Richmond to compete with whites,
Ashe moves to St. Louis—where he becomes the fifth-ranked junior in
the nation.

1963 First black player named to the U.S. Davis Cup team.

1966 Graduates from UCLA with a degree in business administration.

1968 Wins the U.S. Open—the only black man to hold the title. Believing that responsibilities come with success, Ashe dedicates himself to dismantling the barriers of poverty, privilege, and racism. Creates the Junior Tennis league, a program designed to develop inner-city tennis players.

1973 The first black athlete to be granted a visa (but not hotel accommodations) in apartheid South Africa, Ashe is also the first black pro to play in their championship. Two years later he wins Wimbledon, another first: the only black man to win the world's prestigious grass-court title. The Grand Slam titles net Ashe $1.5 million in prize money, establishing him as tennis's first black millionaire.

1977 Marries photographer Jeanne Moutoussamy. U.S. Ambassador Andrew Young presides at their United Nations wedding.

1980 Fifty-one titles later, Ashe retires from competitive tennis. He becomes captain of the Davis Cup team, but has heart trouble, and three years later undergoes double-bypass surgery.

1985 Arrested outside the South African embassy during an antiapartheid protest.

1988 Hospitalized for numbness in his right hand, Ashe finds out he has HIV—received from his blood transfusion five years earlier. Not wanting to lead a one-issue life, protective of his family's privacy, Ashe chooses not to broadcast his condition. Later that year, his three-volume history, *A Hard Road to Glory: A History of the African Athlete,* hits bookstores.

1992 Believing *USA Today* is about to report his health status, Ashe calls a press conference himself and makes the announcement: he has AIDS. It is the beginning of his life as an AIDS activist. Militant in his convictions but mild in manner, the bookish, bespectacled Ashe doesn't think of himself as a rebel—preferring information to insurrection. On World AIDS Day, he addresses the United Nations, imploring delegates to increase funding for research. Establishes namesake foundation to fight AIDS. *Sports Illustrated* names him Sportsman of the Year.

1993 Dies of AIDS-related pneumonia in New York. His body is transported to the governor's mansion in Richmond—the first person to lie in state at the mansion since Stonewall Jackson in 1863—and his funeral is attended by thousands. Three years later on what would have been his 53rd birthday, a statue of Ashe is erected in Richmond, carrying books in one hand and a tennis racket in the other.

CHARLES ATLAS

By Jerry Cowle, longtime admirer

WRITTEN IN COMMEMORATION

The recent interest in bodybuilding has brought to my mind my boyhood and my encounter with the patron saint of the art of obsession, Charles Atlas. As a scrawny kid of eleven, living in a small upstate New York town, I was an enthusiastic reader of *The Shadow,* Doc Savage and the sports pulp magazines, most of which carried the Charles Atlas ads, but I never dreamed I'd ever meet the great man himself. How could that godlike being ever have been a ninety-seven-pound weakling? And what was this Dynamic Tension that changed his life?

You can imagine my delight when my mother brought home a brochure for Camp Atlas with my hero depicted on the cover. The camp was on a lake in the Catskills, and the brochure promised that

Mr. Atlas would be in attendance all summer. My mother enrolled my brother and me for the full season.

Camp Atlas was much the same as any other camp. It had cabins, double-decker bunks, a mess hall, baseball fields, volleyball courts, a dock, boats, canoes. The campers all wore uniforms and called the counselors Uncle. The difference was Charles Atlas. And he was there all summer, as promised. So were his wife and son. His son's name was—are you ready for this?—Hercules. We called him Herk.

The first evening, we gathered in the mess hall to meet Charles Atlas. He appeared dressed in a leopard-skin loincloth. He was big and bronzed, with rippling muscles and wavy hair. The campers all went wild. "He's real!" the kid next to me said.

Atlas welcomed us in a quiet, friendly voice. He told us what he would like to accomplish with us during the summer, how he hoped that every camper would improve his physique. Then he gave a demonstration of his strength. First he tore a Manhattan phone book in half. Next he bent an iron bar into a horseshoe shape with his bare hands. Then he gripped a long iron bar in his teeth and had two men hang from it, one from each end, until it bent under their weight. Finally he lay on a bed of nails while the same two men stood on a board across his chest. We all cheered like crazy.

Atlas was a beautiful specimen compared to today's muscle men. No gruesome knots, no grotesque, overdeveloped pectorals, simply a man who had harmoniously developed his body. He was well-deserving of the title "World's Most Perfectly Developed Man." His system of bodybuilding, Dynamic Tension, was what we now call isometrics, except that Atlas advocated pitting one set of muscles against another. He didn't approve of gadgets. He believed you were less likely to hurt yourself or "overdo it" when only your own strength was involved.

The encounter with Atlas that I best recall took place when my age group had a special awards campfire, and he came to present the medals. Afterward, he sat in the midst of our group and called for questions.

"How did you ever get started," one kid asked.

"Believe it or not," Atlas said, "I really was a ninety-seven-pound weakling. And very sickly. When I was twenty, a doctor told me not to walk up even one flight of stairs because it might kill me." He paused. "But I knew I couldn't stand living that way, so I ran up three flights!"

"And then what happened?" another kid asked.

"Well, I'm still here!" We all laughed. "After that I began to believe I could do anything if I wanted to badly enough. That's when I started eating right, exercising and developing my system."

I don't know where I got my nerve, but I asked, "Is Charles Atlas your real name?" I'd been reading about Greek mythology.

He looked me straight in the eye, and I felt like sinking into the ground. "My real name is Angelo Siciliano," he said. "I borrowed Atlas from the Greeks, and now my legal name is Charles S. Atlas."

Emboldened, I asked him if there was a special rate for his mail course for kids who had attended Camp Atlas. "I never thought about that," he said. "What's your name, son?" I told him. "Well, Jerry, after you get home and write me and remind me. I'll give you a 50 percent discount on the course." (After camp, I did write him. Sure enough he answered, offering the entire series for $10, or half price. To save postage, Atlas sent all the lessons at once. I put them away, using one each week just as though they were coming in the mail.)

Because Hercules Atlas was my age, he often joined our group for sports and other activities. He was a quiet boy who seemed embarrassed by his name. We eyed him with a certain amount of awe, wondering if his father had endowed Hercules with superhuman strength.

Charles Atlas led us in calisthenics every morning before breakfast. Later he would roam the mess hall, making sure we ate the foods that would help us build our bodies. When one boy left his bread crust on the plate, Atlas picked it up and ate it. "That's the best part of the bread," he told the kid. I'm sure that was the last crust the boy ever left. By the end of the summer, most of us had developed a great affection for this fantastic man, admiring him as much for his kind manner as for his physique. But the next year, I was old enough to go to Boy Scout camp, so I never saw Camp Atlas again. Or any of my fellow campers—except one.

Many years later, when I was an ensign in the U.S. Coast Guard, preparing for the invasion of Normandy, we tied up next to a Navy LCI in Southampton Harbor, England. One evening, returning from liberty, I started a conversation with a young ensign on the Navy ship. He invited me into the wardroom for coffee. "My name is Charles Atlas," he said. "Junior," he added, when I looked startled.

I looked at him carefully. Could it be . . . ? Yes, there was a resemblance. "When you were younger, was your name Hercules?"

You'd have thought he'd seen a ghost. "How did you know?"

"I was at Camp Atlas. A long time ago."

He looked at me closely. "Yes . . . Camp Atlas. Weren't you the kid who always wanted to play shortstop?"

I was. So we spent some time reminiscing about that summer. He told me he'd changed his name to Charles Jr. I didn't have to ask why. We hit it off well.

The next morning, he was on deck to supervise the casting of our mooring lines. As we stood out to sea, he waved goodbye, and that was the last time I ever saw him. I've occasionally wondered how he and his ship made out in the invasion, and what he ended up doing after the war. [In fact, he teaches math at Lincoln Junior High School in Santa Monica, California.]

Around Christmas 1972, I came across a newspaper account of the death of Charles Atlas. I found it hard to accept. To me, he would always look the way he did that summer, standing in front of the campers in his loincloth, performing feats of strength and making a bunch of little kids believe that each of us could grow up to be just like him.

1893 Born Angelo Siciliano, in Calabria, Italy.

1903 Spindly 10-year-old Angelo arrives at Ellis Island along with thousands of other immigrants. As a youth, he is frequently beaten up by Brooklyn school bullies.

1910 "One day I went to Coney Island and I had a very pretty girl with me. We were sitting on the sand. A big, husky lifeguard, maybe there were two of them, kicked sand in my face." Thus begins his makeover into barrel-chested hero. Watching a lion at the zoo, Angelo realizes the lion's apparent stretches are powerful muscular development exercises— then uses the same means to change himself from 97-lb. weakling into the most physically advanced human alive.

1915 New measurements: 5-feet-10 and 180 lbs. Biceps: 17 inches. Chest: 47 inches. Waist: 32 inches. Transformation complete, Angelo, enters fitness competitions. Models for artists. And assumes "Strongman" role at Coney Island Circus.

1922 Winning "Most Perfectly Developed Man" contest at Madison Square Garden, he changes his name to Charles Atlas. All plans for further MSG competitions are cancelled. "What's the use? Atlas will win every time."

1924 Publishes his fitness health course.

1928 Teams up with legendary adman Charles Roman. Together they launch the "sand in the face" ad campaign, and within months they are millionaires. Legs planted in white sand, Atlas asks for a five-day trial to turn a spindly youth into a tower of strength. The course sells for $30 and goes out in seven languages to over 70,000 people/year. Three generations of comics will carry his ad.

1930 Atlas's star continues to rise. Appearing in countless magazines, news shows, and newspapers, he becomes renowned for feats of strength. During a storm, he swims out to a floundering boat and tows it back to shore with a rope.

1938 And another: Pulls a 145,000-pound railroad car through the Sunnyside yards of Pennsylvania Railroad, moving the car 122 feet with a single rope.

1950 The American Medical Association enthusiastically endorses his Dynamic Tension course.

1972 Dies in Long Beach, age 79, after his daily jog on the beach—having helped millions of little guys by keeping beaches safe all around the world.

WILT CHAMBERLAIN

By Barbara Chamberlain Lewis, sister

DELIVERED AT MEMORIAL SERVICE, OCTOBER 16, 1999
CITY OF ANGELS CHURCH, LOS ANGELES

Oh, what they said about Dip—I don't call him Wilt, he's known as "Dip" in our family. You all know him as Wilt Chamberlain and Wilt the Stilt. The only person that called him Wilton was my mother. Everyone else called him the Dipper, the Dip.

I don't know what to say that would take less than three hours, but the Chamberlains are known for talking a lot, and he was the biggest talker of them all. (Except for my sister Margaret. I hope you're not listening to this, Margaret.)

He thought nothing about calling you at two or three o'clock in the morning. "Well, you're not sleeping, Babs. And I got a lot on my mind."

"Well, so do I."

"Listen, let's do a book!"

"A book on what?"

A book for kids. Let's do this. Let's do that. He was so busy doing. I'm not surprised he had a tired heart—he gave so much of it to us. He was such a great brother and son.

He came across like he was such a big bad guy, but believe me, he never shouted in our house. None of us were allowed to shout. If Dip did, he kept it outside of Olivia's ears—my mother didn't play that game. My father didn't raise his voice, and they weren't ever allowed to raise theirs. So when he did all his "talking" he made sure they were gone.

He was a worker. Always a worker. Can you imagine a five-year-old kid sneaking outside at five o'clock in the morning to help the ice man, the milkman, the rag man?

My mother said, "Wilton, what are you doing? You're just five years old!"

"But I'm strong, Mom, I'm strong and I'm smart. I'm gonna make me a lot of money one day. And I can't stay in bed. I got things I gotta do!"

Five years old. Ask any neighbor, he always had a job to do. Always tried to give you a job, too . . .

"Mom, I think I can fix food better than you can."

"I don't think so, son!" But he'd watch her. He wanted to be the best cook. And you know he played cards and cheated like a dawg, but he swore he didn't. My father was a great cardsman and a five-foot-seven-inch man, but he was the giant in our house. Dip was just Dip.

Those were the days when you didn't lock doors, and you better not look like a nigger, or speak like one. Those were the days when you'd better not say anything because someone would tell your mother. Dip was never a giant in that house.

My mother was close to six feet. She and my dad were the giants.

And they didn't raise their voices. Come dinnertime: "You see me standing here? When you see me standing here, I want you in this house!" So we looked for her. We stood on the corner and looked for her. Of course, Dip would try to be slick and pretend he didn't see her. He'd try to contest her.

He would say things, and my mother would say, "I don't want you talking to people like that. I want you to keep your mouth quiet. You talk too much!"

Come breakfast: "Mom, why is that lady coming to our house to eat every day? I am so tired of that lady. Every morning she comes to our house, every Sunday she knows you're fixing that big breakfast after church"—and I'm not gonna say the woman's name but we all know who she is—and she would say, "Oh Mrs. Chamberlain, you set such a beautiful table. You expecting guests?"

She lived down the street. She knew we weren't expecting guests.

And Wilt would be punching me, because we sat at the table in age order, and it was all I could do to say, "Don't you say anything!"

He'd say, "I'm going to tell this woman one day. She says the same thing every Sunday: 'Did you make those biscuits yourself? Oh, is that syrup? Oh, chicken and liver and sausage! All that for your kids?'"

"Well, I've got nine kids," my mother would say, "and I'm taking care of three others, and I've got you here every Sunday."

Well, Dip thought that was his clue to speak up, too.

"Yeah, you're here every Sunday. Every Sunday! And you start off with 'Oh those biscuits look good,' and you end up with 'Can I have a little something just to take the sweetness out of my mouth. How about three more eggs?'"

We really only had a dozen eggs, but Mother put a half a pound of cheese in it, and a quart of milk, I'm sure. Whipped it up with a fork and put it on a platter, and it looked like we had a lot of eggs. We thought we had a lot of food. And we did.

We thought we had a lot of gifts. We did. We had the gift of love. We had *such* a gift of love.

And that gift spread right through him.

He ended up being a giving, loving, big-mouthed person.

1936 Born in Philadelphia—one of nine children —to parents neither of whom are bigger than 5'10".

1951 Shoots up to 6'11" by the time he enters Overbrook High. An avid basketball player, Wilt draws national attention for his school. Later becomes the most coveted student recruit, sought after by more than 200 colleges before he settles on University of Kansas.

1959 Leaves Kansas to join the Harlem Globetrotters. Salary: $65,000. Plays for the Philadelphia Warriors for six years. When the team is sold to San Francisco, he stays on—eventually returning to Philly to play for the '76ers. "The Big Dipper" leads in point production, but believes his height limits his popularity. "Nobody roots for Goliath," he claims, but goes on to win both MVP and Rookie of the Year.

1961 The NBA changes its rules, widening the lane specifically to keep Chamberlain further from the basket. During his NBA career, remarkably, he never once fouls out of the game—despite being the centerpiece on defense.

1962 Shatters record for most points in a game: 100.

1966 Flirts with other sports, including boxing, track and field, volleyball, and auto racing. The AFL offers him a pro football contract. But his heart is in basketball, and the following year he leads the '76ers to the NBA championship. Fodder for the press is his long-standing (but good-natured) rivalry with Boston Celtic Bill Russell—fierce competitors on the court, yet close personal friends off the hardwood.

1968 Joins the L.A. Lakers.

1973 Swansong: Chamberlain retires, leaving the game with a total of 31,419 points—a record later broken by Kareem Abdul-Jabbar. Even after he hangs up his size-16 sneakers, Chamberlain remains a high-profile, highly quotable man.

1979 Inducted into the Basketball Hall of Fame.

1991 Publishes a revealing autobiography, *A View from Above*—famously claiming to have had sex with over 20,000 women. Facing heavy criticism, Chamberlain responds, "I was just doing what was natural—chasing good-looking ladies, whoever they were and wherever they were available." The lifelong bachelor later tells the press, "The women who I have been the most attracted to, the most in love with, I've pushed away the strongest."

1999 Dies of a heart attack in his sleep, age 63—a center so big he forced basketball to change its rules.

CHRISTY MATHEWSON

By John McGraw, team manager and best friend

DELIVERED AT FUNERAL, OCTOBER 9, 1925
LEWISBURG, PENNSYLVANIA

In laying Christy Mathewson to rest today, we have paid our last public respect to a great man and a great character. Very likely, I knew Mathewson better than any other man. He began his baseball career with me and finished it with me. From an awkward kid, I watched him grow into the most finished artist in the world.

I never expect to see another such pitcher as Mathewson. He had strength, intellect, and an uncanny memory. Mathewson's real greatness to the game lay in examples he set for young fellows and the impression he left on the minds of the public.

He gave our profession a dignity that it needed and was slow to acquire. Matty had a studious mind. He fully realized his early faults and worked constantly to overcome them. He never looked

270

on his baseball playing as a joke. He encouraged the other players to take things seriously and in that way he was a wonderful example. Only a baseball manager can appreciate what a help that was.

Early in his playing days he appreciated the necessity of absolute discipline. Though a star and a hero to the public, Matty never allowed that to influence him. He did not want to be regarded as a hero. By observing the smallest detail in discipline, he influenced the younger players to do so. Their reaction was that if the great Mathewson had to observe and obey rules, they certainly could not disregard them.

Christy Mathewson had a natural dignity that did much to raise the morals of his teammates. He influenced them to look upon baseball as an honorable profession—one that required skill and constant appreciation. At the same time, Matty was a man's man and had as much fun as anybody. His attitude was never that of a teacher. Somehow he really was a most valuable instructor by example. He loved any game that required cleverness and skill, and was an expert at all of them—checkers, bridge, or chess. I have seen him play eight opponents at checkers simultaneously and never miss a play. His memory was so perfect that he could beat the average good checker player blindfolded. Even after he had become a great star, Mathewson would go out and work for an hour at a time to perfect control of a certain pitching delivery. He never forgot the weakness of any opposing batter.

Capt. Eddie Grant, who was killed in France and who formerly was a major league player, used to tell of the first day he faced Mathewson and got five hits. Eddie for a day or so regarded Matty as easy to hit. But he didn't get another hit that season off Matty. Mathewson undoubtedly was an inspiration to the whole sport of baseball, but he was an even greater inspiration to the players. Knowing that he would do the right thing at all times, players worked behind him with absolute confidence.

His sense of responsibility was so strongly developed that it was almost impossible for him to make thoughtless mistakes. As he grew into greatness, Matty realized that the public expected him to continue great.

He felt a keen responsibility to that public. Mathewson approached any situation seriously and gave it careful study. Much like Walter Johnson, who followed him as a public hero, Matty prepared himself with great care. He was always in good physical condition. For example, he always carried his suitcase in his left hand so as to save the right. By perfecting control, he saved himself much exertion and also steadied the team.

I do not expect to see the like of Mathewson again, but I do know that the example he set and the imprint he left on the sport that he loved and honored will remain long after I have gone. Mathewson was my close friend. His passing is one of the greatest sorrows of my life. God rest his soul.

1880 Born into a wealthy family in Factoryville, Pa.

1898 Attends Bucknell University—where he (1) is elected class president, (2) rushes in two fraternities, (3) letters in football, (4) sings in the glee club, (5) belongs to two literary societies, (6) plays baseball, and (7) generally serves as a model of clean living.

1901 Signs with a Virginia league as pitcher, and catches the attention of the New York Giants. They buy him out of his contract for $1,500. But he loses the next three games—causing the Giants to send him back to Virginia, declare the deal dead, and demand their money back. "You can learn little from victory. You can learn everything from defeat," Mathewson opines.

1902 Traded back to the Giants, he finds his stride. Demonstrating remarkable control of the mound, he throws on 75 to 80 pitches and breezes through games.

1903 Marries Jane Stoughton of Lewisburg, Pa.

1905 The World Series turns him into a star. By now, Mathewson is the dominant pitcher of his era—going on to win 373 games, strike out 2,502 batters, and lead the league in wins four times during his 17-year career.

1906 Christy Mathewson, Jr., is born.

1908 Wins 37 games in a season, a National League record that still stands.

1910 Performs on the vaudeville circuit with teammate John "Chief" Meyers and actress May Tulley for a reported $1,000/week. Publishes his first book, *Won in the Ninth.* The following year, he travels to Cuba on a baseball tour.

1912 His second book, *Pitching in a Pinch,* hits bookstores.

1913 In a time when baseball is known for its hard-living, hard-drinking players, Mathewson is on a literary roll, writing *Pitcher Pollack,* followed by *Catcher Craig, First Base Faulkner* and *Second Base Sloane*—a series of baseball books for kids. "A boy cannot begin playing ball too early. I might almost say that while he is still creeping on all fours, he should have a bouncing rubber ball."

1916 Traded to the Cincinnati Reds, he becomes the team's manager.

1918 During WWI, Mathewson enlists in the army—where he is gassed, with critical repercussions, during a training exercise.

1921 Diagnosed with tuberculosis and given six months to live, Mathewson fights the disease to return to a normal, lower-capacity life. The TB goes into remission.

1925 Suffers a relapse when he is caught and soaked by a fast-moving rain-storm during spring training. Dies in Saranac Lake, N.Y., age of 45, on the opening day of the season—one of the first five legends inducted into the Baseball Hall of Fame, alongside Babe Ruth, Honus Wagner, Ty Cobb, and Walter Johnson.

PARENTS

COL. DON CONROY

By Pat Conroy, son

DELIVERED AT FUNERAL, MAY 14, 1998
BEAUFORT, SOUTH CAROLINA

The children of fighter pilots tell different stories than other kids do. None of our fathers can write a will or sell a life insurance policy or fill out a prescription or administer a flu shot or explain what a poet meant. We tell of fathers who land on aircraft carriers at pitch-black night with the wind howling out of the China Sea. Our fathers wiped out aircraft batteries in the Philippines and set Japanese soldiers on fire when they made the mistake of trying to overwhelm our troops on the ground.

Your dads ran the barber shops and worked at the post office and delivered the packages on time and sold the cars, while our dads were blowing up fuel depots near Seoul, were providing extraordinarily courageous close air support to the beleaguered Marines at the Chosin Reservoir, and who once turned the Naktong River red with blood of a retreating North Korean battalion.

We tell of men who made widows of the wives of our nations' enemies and who made orphans out of all their children. You don't like war or violence? Or napalm? Or rockets? Or cannons or death rained down from the sky? Then let's talk about your fathers, not ours. When we talk about the aviators who raised us and the Marines who loved us, we can look you in the eye and say, "You would not like to have been America's enemies when our fathers passed overhead." We were raised by the men who made the United States of America the safest country on earth in the bloodiest century in all recorded history. Our fathers made sacred those strange, singing names of battlefields across the Pacific: Guadalcanal, Iwo Jima, Okinawa, the Chosin Reservoir, Khe Sanh, and a thousand more. We grew up attending the funerals of Marines slain in these battles. Your fathers made communities like Beaufort decent and prosperous and functional; our fathers made the world safe for democracy.

We have gathered here today to celebrate the amazing and storied life of Col. Donald Conroy, who modestly called himself by his nom de guerre, the Great Santini. There should be no sorrow at this funeral because the Great Santini lived life at full throttle, moved always in the fast lanes, gunned every engine, teetered on every edge, seized every moment and shook it like a terrier shaking a rat. He did not know what moderation was or where you'd go to look for it.

Donald Conroy is the only person I have ever known whose self-esteem was absolutely unassailable. There was not one thing about himself that my father did not like, nor was there one thing about himself that he would change. He simply adored the man he was and walked with perfect confidence through every encounter in his life. Dad wished everyone could be just like him. His stubbornness was an art form. The Great Santini did what he did, when he wanted to do it, and woe to the man who got in his way.

Once I introduced my father before he gave a speech to an Atlanta audience. I said at the end of the introduction, "My father decided to go into the Marine Corps on the day he discovered his IQ was the temperature of this room."

My father rose to the podium, stared down at the audience, and said without skipping a beat, "My God, it's hot in here! It must be at least 180 degrees."

Here is how my father appeared to me as a boy. He came from a race of giants and demigods from a mythical land known as Chicago. He married the most beautiful girl ever to come crawling out of the poor and lowborn South, and there were times when I thought we were being raised by Zeus and Athena.

After Happy Hour my father would drive his car home at a hundred miles an hour to see his wife and seven children. He would get out of his car, a strapping flight-jacketed matinee idol, and walk toward his house, his knuckles dragging along the ground, his shoes stepping on and killing small animals in his slouching amble toward the home place. My sister, Carol, stationed at the door, would call out, "Godzilla's home!" and we seven children would scamper toward the door to watch his entry. The door would be flung open and the strongest Marine aviator on earth would shout, "Stand by for a fighter pilot!"

He would then line his seven kids up against the wall and say, "Who's the greatest of them all?"

"You are, O Great Santini, you are."

"Who knows all, sees all, and hears all?"

"You do, O Great Santini, you do."

We were not in the middle of a normal childhood, yet none of us were sure since it was the only childhood we would ever have. For all we knew, other men were coming home and shouting to their families, "Stand by for a pharmacist," or "Stand by for a chiropractor."

In the old, bewildered world of children, we knew we were in the presence of a fabulous, overwhelming personality; but had no idea we were being raised by a genius of his own myth-making. My mother always told me that my father had reminded her of Rhett Butler on the day they met, and everyone who ever knew our mother conjured up the lovely, coquettish image of Scarlett O'Hara.

Let me give you my father the warrior in full battle array. The Great Santini is catapulted off the deck of the aircraft carrier *Sicily*. His Black Sheep squadron is the first to reach the Korean Theater, and American ground troops had been getting torn up by North Korean regulars. Let me do it in his voice:

"We didn't even have a map of Korea. Not zip. We just headed toward the sound of artillery firing along the Naktong River. They told us to keep the North Koreans on their side of the Naktong. Air power hadn't been a factor until we got there that day. I radioed to Bill Lundin—I was his wingman: 'There they are. Let's go get 'em.' So we did."

I was interviewing Dad, so I asked, "How do you know you got them?"

"Easy," the Great Santini said. "They were running—it's a good sign when you see the enemy running. There was another good sign."

"What was that, Dad?"

"They were on fire."

This is the world in which my father lived deeply. I had no knowledge of it as a child. When I was writing the book *The Great Santini*, they told me at Headquarters Marines that Don Conroy was at one time one of the most decorated aviators in the Marine Corps. I did not know he had won a single medal. When his children gathered together to write his obituary, not one of us knew of any medal he had won, but he had won a slew of them.

When he flew back toward the carrier that day, he received a call from an Army colonel on the ground who had witnessed the route of the North Koreans across the river. "Could you go pass over the troops fifty miles south of here? They've been catching hell for a week or more. It'd do them good to know you flyboys are around."

He flew those fifty miles and came over a mountain and saw a thousand troops lumbered down in foxholes. He and Bill Lundin went in low so these troops could read the insignias and know the American aviators had entered the fray. My father said, "Thousands of guys came screaming out of their foxholes, son. It sounded like a World Series game. I got goose pimples in the cockpit. Get goose pimples telling it forty-eight years later. I dipped my wings, waved to the guys. The roar they let out. I hear it now. I hear it now."

During the Cuban Missile Crisis, my mother took me out to the air station, where we watched Dad's squadron scramble on the runway on their bases at Roosevelt Road and Guantanamo.

In the car as we watched the A-4's take off, my mother began to say the rosary.

"You praying for Dad and his men, Mom?" I asked her.

"No, son. I'm praying for the repose of the souls of the Cuban pilots they're going to kill."

Later I would ask my father what his squadron's mission was during the Missile Crisis. "To clear the air of MIGs over Cuba," he said.

"You think you could've done it?"

The Great Santini answered, "There wouldn't have been a bluebird flying over that island, son."

Now let us turn to the literary history of *The Great Santini*. Some of you may have heard that I had some serious reservations about my father's child-rearing practices. When *The Great Santini* came out, the book roared through my family like a nuclear device. My father hated it; my grandparents hated it; my aunts and uncles hated it; my cousins who adore my father thought I was a psychopath for writing it; and rumor has it that my mother gave it to the judge in her divorce case and said, "It's all there. Everything you need to know."

What changed my father's mind was when Hollywood entered the picture and wanted to make a movie of it. This is when my father said, "What a shame John Wayne is dead. Now there was a man. Only he could've gotten my incredible virility across to the American people."

Orion Pictures did me a favor and sent my father a telegram: "Dear Col. Conroy: We have selected the actor to play you in the coming film. He wants to come to Atlanta to interview you. His name is Truman Capote."

But my father took well to Hollywood and its Byzantine, unspeakable ways. When his movie came out, he began reading *Variety* on a daily basis. He called the movie a classic the first month of its existence. He claimed that he had a place in the history of film. In February of the following year, he burst into my apartment in Atlanta, as excited as I have ever seen him, and screamed, "Son, you and I were nominated for Academy Awards last night. Your mother didn't get squat."

Ladies and gentlemen, you are attending the funeral of the most famous Marine that ever lived. Dad's life had grandeur, majesty, and sweep. We were all caught in the middle of living lives much paler and less daring than the Great Santini's. His was a high-stepping, damn-the-torpedoes kind of life, and the stick was always set at high throttle. There is not another Marine alive who has not heard of the Great Santini. There's not a fighter pilot alive who does not lift his glass whenever Don Conroy's name is mentioned and give the fighter-pilot toast: "Hurrah for the next man to die."

One day last summer, my father asked me to drive him over to Beaufort National Cemetery. He wanted to make sure there were no administrative foul-ups about his plot. I could think of more pleasurable ways to spend the afternoon, but Dad brought new eloquence to the word *stubborn*. We went into the office and a pretty black woman said that everything was squared away.

My father said, "It'll be the second time I've been buried in this cemetery." The woman and I both looked strangely at Dad. Then he explained: "You ever catch the flick *The Great Santini*? That was me they planted at the end of the movie."

All of you will be part of a very special event today. You will be witnessing the actual burial that has already been filmed in fictional setting. This has never happened in world history. You will be present in a scene that was acted out in film in 1979. You will be in the same town and the same cemetery. Only the Great Santini himself will be different.

In his last weeks my father told me, "I was always your best subject, son. Your career took a nose dive after *The Great Santini* came out." He had become so media savvy that during his last illness he told me not to schedule his funeral on the same day as the *Seinfeld* farewell.

The Colonel thought it would hold down the crowd. The Colonel's death was front-page news across the country. CNN announced his passing on the evening news all around the world.

Don Conroy was a simple man and an American hero. His wit was remarkable; his intelligence frightening; and his sophistication next to none. He was a man's man, and I would bet he hadn't spent a thousand dollars in his whole life on his wardrobe. He lived out his whole retirement in a two-room efficiency in the Darlington Apartments in Atlanta. He claimed he never spent over a dollar on any piece of furniture he owned. You would believe him if you saw the furniture.

Dad bought a season ticket for himself to Six Flags Over Georgia and would often go there alone to enjoy the rides and hear the children squeal with pleasure. He was a beer drinker who thought wine was for Frenchmen or effete social climbers like his children.

Ah! His children. Here is how God gets a Marine Corps fighter pilot. He sends him seven squirrelly, mealy-mouth children who march in peace demonstrations, wear Birkenstocks, flirt with vegetarianism, invite cross-dressers to dinner, and vote for candidates that Dad would line up and shoot. If my father knew how many tears his children had shed since his death, he would be mortally ashamed of us all and begin yelling that he should've been tougher on us all, knocked us into better shape—that he certainly didn't mean to raise a passel of kids so weak and tacky they would cry at his death. Don Conroy was the best uncle I ever saw, the best brother, the best grandfather, the best friend—and my God, what a father.

After my mother divorced him and *The Great Santini* was published, Don Conroy had the best second act I ever saw. He never was simply a father.

This was the Great Santini.

It is time to leave you, Dad. From Carol and Mike and Kathy and Jim and Tim and especially from Tom. Your kids wanted to especially thank Katy and Bobby and Willie Harvey who cared for you heroically. Let us leave you and say goodbye, Dad, with the passwords that bind all Marines and their wives and their children forever. The Corps was always the most important thing.

Semper Fi, Dad.

Semper Fi, O Great Santini.

HILDA STEGNER

By Wallace Stegner, son

Mom, listen.

In three months I will be eighty years old, thirty years older than you were when you died, twenty years older than my father was when he died, fifty-seven years older than my brother was when he died. I got the genes and the luck. The rest of you have been gone for a long time.

Except when I have to tie my shoelaces, I don't feel eighty years old. I—the sickly child—have outlasted you all. But if I don't feel decrepit, neither do I feel wise and confident. Age and experience have not made me a Nestor qualified to tell others how to live their lives. I feel more like Theodore Dreiser, who confessed that he would depart from life more bewildered than he had arrived in it.

Instead of being embittered, or stoical, or calm, or resigned, or any of the standard things that a long life might have made me, I confess that I am simply lost, as much in need of comfort, understanding forgiveness, uncritical love—the things you used to give me—as I ever was at five, or ten, or fifteen.

Fifty-five years ago, sitting up with you after midnight while the nurse rested, I watched you take your last breath. A few minutes before you died you half-raised your head and said, "Which . . . way?" I understood that: you were at a dark, unmarked crossing. Then a minute later you said, "You're a good . . . boy . . . Wallace," and died.

My name was the last word you spoke; your faith in me and love for me were your last thoughts. I could bear them no better than I could bear your death, and I went blindly out into the November darkness and walked for hours with my mind clenched like a fist.

I knew how far from true your last words were. There had been plenty of times when I had not been a good boy or a thoughtful one. I knew you could no longer see my face, that you spoke from a clouded, drugged dream, that I had already faded to a memory that you clung to even while you waned from life. I knew that it was the love speaking, not you, that you had already gone, that your love lasted longer than you yourself did. And I had some dim awareness that as you went away you laid on me an immense and unavoidable obligation. I would never get over trying, however badly or sadly or confusedly, to be what you thought I was.

Obviously you did not die. Death is a convention, a certification to the end of pain, something for the vital-statistics book, not binding on anyone but the keepers of the graveyard records. For as I sit at the desk, trying to tell you something fifty-five years too late, I have a clear mental image of your pursed lips and your crinkling eyes, and I know that nothing I can say will persuade you that I was ever less than you thought of me. Your kind of love, once given, is never lost. You are alive and luminous in my head. Except when I fail to listen, you will speak through me when I face some crisis of feeling or sympathy or consideration of others. You are a curb on my natural impatience and competitiveness and arrogance. When I have been less than myself, you make me ashamed even as you forgive me. You're a good . . . boy . . . Wallace . . .

EDITH FREUNDLICH

By Peter Freundlich, son

DELIVERED AT FUNERAL, MAY 30, 2004
RIVERSIDE MEMORIAL CHAPEL, NEW YORK CITY

I think of this as a reunion. My mother first met death a long time ago, at a couple of concentration camps in Germany. The two of them spent every minute together for months, were intimate in unimaginable ways, shared a wooden shelf at night and what little there was to eat, or, more often, went hungry together for days, trudged about in the cold and mud, became a single being almost—and then, finally, parted company. Death decided—to her everlasting amazement—that although it wanted a great many others she knew and loved, and millions more she knew about but had never met, it did not, after all that, want her. This puzzled and angered her forever.

Joy came afterward in her life. She was reunited with my father, and had a fifty-year-long marriage to him. To call her devoted is to understate the case. He was the air she breathed; it has been almost literally hard for her to inhale ever since he died ten years ago. And she more than loved, we all more than loved, her wonderful younger brother, who is also gone now. That disappearance was especially terrible for her, coming as it did out of order. She surely expected him to survive her.

God knows she loved my brother Andy and me, and our partners. And she was dizzy about our kids—Keith and Jenny and Jessica and Nick. There are quite a few people in this city her grandchildren themselves don't know from Adam who nonetheless know *them,* thanks to my mother's bragging. They are *so* smart, *so* sweet, *so* funny, *so* tall, *so* grown up: Think of a good thing and put the word *so* in front of it. That was her asssement of her grandchildren.

I could eat them up, is what she used to say. A lot.

The point is that there was great joy in her life . . . joy, comfort, love, much hard work, well-tended connections to a world that was no more. Especially in the last few years, that was her central preoccupation—remembering. There seemed to be candles to light every day. Her calendar was clotted with anniversaries. Every conversation with her eventually came down to some tiny crystal-clear recollection of the perished, like a little snow globe of sadness it helped her to look into.

Oh, and she was vain, with reason, because she was good-looking and elegant and knew it. She was very fond of admiration, the more unreserved the better, and of attention, the more undivided the better. And then, especially in the last decade or so, she was terribly easily bruised: A sharp word, a raised voice, a cross look would be enough to wound her for weeks. I was particularly stupid in this regard—dense almost—and spent a lot of time apologizing. My last e-mail from her, a couple of days ago—yes, she mastered e-mail at the age of eighty—was yet another acceptance of an apology from me. It said, in its entirety, all in caps and with a bunch of typos, because her keyboard work was rather spotty: "I was hurt but it is all gone now. I love you forever and ever. Your Mom and more."

But Death had extracted an IOU from her almost sixty years ago, and she never forgot that, not for a day. Sometimes I wonder whether so much as an hour went by without the thought popping into her head. Finally, on Friday, after leaving her wondering and waiting for an entire long lifetime, after peeking out from behind every one of the many happinesses she had, after plucking everyone else from just beside her and just behind her, Death at last showed up for her, while she was sleeping in her chair, her TV table in front of her, with a full glass of orange juice on it and a little mosaic of the many pills she took all laid out and ready on a paper towel. Death took her—as she deserved—neatly and politely and respectfully, disturbing nothing else around her, nothing at all, not the juice, not the pills, not the thick pillows behind her in the chair. In that quiet, immaculate room, nothing else was moved, nothing else was touched—except her.

I deeply hope that the settlement of this old debt has brought my mother the peace she should have had long ago. And I hope that she is reunited now with all those—there were so many—with whom she should have spent many more years than she was given the chance by that willful, on-again, off-again figure who first made a claim on her before any of us here were born, and then teased and teased and teased her until just the other day.

Acknowledgments

My editor, Chuck Adams, at Algonquin—a gentleman. My agent, Mary Evans—a cultured warrior. Larry Gelbart, for his elegiac contributions to the art form. My friends who keep my spirits afloat even as I traffic in goodbyes. Lee Bantle, in whose large heart a world could take refuge. The life-sharing and fiercely beautiful Copeland Women—touchstones both. And my father, whom I still miss a decade later. Delivering his eulogy started me on this journey.

Credits and Permissions

Movie Stars

Bette Davis eulogy by David Hartman courtesy of David Hartman, with kind assistance from Kathryn Sermak.

Judy Garland eulogy by James Mason courtesy of Morgan Mason.

Marilyn Monroe eulogy by Donald Spoto courtesy of Donald Spoto.

Charlie Chaplin eulogy by Jerry Epstein courtesy of Dr. Susan Brand and Frank Scheide at University of Arkansas. Originally appeared in *Remembering Charlie* by Jerry Epstein.

Joan Crawford eulogy by George Cukor courtesy of estate of George Cukor.

James Mason eulogy by Nicholas Meyer courtesy of Nicholas Meyer.

Gregory Peck eulogy by Larry Gelbart; © 2004 by Larry Gelbart.

Tallulah Bankhead eulogy by Anita Loos courtesy of Tony Grillo; © 1968 Anita Loos Trust.

Orson Welles eulogy by Charlton Heston courtesy of Charlton Heston.

Pioneers

Princess Diana eulogy by Lord Edward John Spencer.

Julia Child eulogy by Jacques Pépin courtesy of Jacques Pépin (originally appeared in *Food Arts* magazine, October 2004). Julia Child photo courtesy of James Scherer for WGBH/Boston.

Bill W. eulogy by Dr. Jack Norris courtesy of Eleanor Norris and The Wilson House. Bill W. photo courtesy of Alcoholics Anonymous.

Alfred Kinsey eulogy by Helen D'Amico courtesy of Helen D'Amico and The Kinsey Institute. Alfred Kinsey photo by William Dellenback courtesy of The Kinsey Institute for Research in Sex, Gender, and Reproduction, Inc.

Karen Silkwood eulogy and photo courtesy of Michael Meadows.

Sigmund Freud eulogy by Stefan Zweig courtesy of Williams Verlag.

Albert Schweitzer eulogy by Walter Munz courtesy of Walter Munz, previously given at "World Peace Through Reverence for Life" Symposium on October 13, 2000; © 2000 by Walter Munz. Albert Schweitzer photo courtesy of Meghan Kalinic; © 1965 by Meghan Kalinic. Albert Schweitzer Fellowship photo by Erica Anderson.

Elisabeth Kübler-Ross eulogy courtesy of David Kessler. Elisabeth Kübler-Ross photo courtesy of Ken Ross; © 1987, 2005 by Ken Ross.

Media Titans

Edward R. Murrow eulogy by Charles Kuralt originally published in *North Carolina Historical Review,* April 1971; © 1971 by the N.C. Dept. of Archives. Edward R. Murrow photo courtesy of Digital Collections and Archives, Tufts University.

Katharine Graham eulogy by Ben Bradlee courtesy of Ben Bradlee, and *The Washington Post.* Additional assistance from Liz Hylton and Carol Leggett. Katherine Graham photo by Bill King courtesy of Donald E. Graham; © 1971 by Bill King.

Malcolm Forbes eulogy by Steve Forbes courtesy of Steve Forbes and *Forbes* Magazine. Malcolm Forbes photo courtesy of Robert Forbes; © 1977 Robert Forbes/Forbes Archives.

David Brinkley eulogy by Joel Brinkley courtesy of Joel Brinkley. David Brinkley photo courtesy of Joel Brinkley.

Henry Luce eulogy by Robert T. Elson courtesy of R. Anthony Elson, and *Time* Magazine.

Entertainers

Fred Rogers eulogy by Teresa Heinz courtesy of Teresa Heinz. Fred Rogers photo courtesy of Family Communications.

Bob Hope eulogy by Larry Gelbart courtesy of Larry Gelbart; © 2004 Larry Gelbart. Bob Hope photo courtesy of Ward Grant, Bob Hope Enterprises.

John Belushi eulogy by Dan Aykroyd courtesy of Dan Aykroyd.

Walt Disney eulogy by Roy Disney courtesy of Roy Disney. Originally appeared in *Readers Digest* magazine, February 1969. Walt Disney photo courtesy of Howard Green; © 1969 Disney.

Lenny Bruce eulogy by Rev. Howard Moody courtesy of Howard Moody. Originally appeared in *Esquire* magazine, fall 1963. Lenny Bruce photo courtesy of Ben Thum.

Milton Berle eulogy by Larry Gelbart courtesy of Larry Gelbart; © 2004 Larry Gelbart.

Tunesmiths & Troubadours

Leonard Bernstein eulogy by Ned Rorem courtesy of Ned Rorem. Leonard Bernstein photo courtesy of New York Philharmonic archives.

Dusty Springfield eulogy by Neil Tenant courtesy of Neil Tenant; © 1999 Neil Tenant.

Jerry Garcia eulogy by Robert Hunter courtesy of Robert Hunter. Jerry Garcia photo courtesy of Herb Greene; © 1987 Herb Greene.

Cy Coleman eulogy by Larry Gelbart courtesy of Larry Gelbart; © 2004 Larry Gelbart.

John Denver eulogy by Tom Crum courtesy of Tom Crum.

Nina Simone eulogy by Ossie Davis courtesy of Ossie Davis.

9/11 Heroes

Father Mychal Judge eulogy by Father Michael Duffy courtesy of Michael Duffy. Father Mychal Judge photo courtesy of Jim McIntosh and Phillip Jacobs for *The Anthonian;* © 2001 *The Anthonian.*

Capt. Robert Dolan eulogy by Mark Wallinger courtesy of Mark Wallinger. Originally appeared on Smithsonian Institute and Museum Web site. Photo courtesy of Lisa Dolan.

Chief Peter Ganci eulogy by Chris Ganci courtesy of Chris Ganci. Chief Peter Ganci photo courtesy of Kathleen Ganci and the FDNY.

Capt. Francis Callahan eulogy by Capt. James Gormley courtesy of James

Gormley. Originally appeared in *The New York Times Week in Review,* December 23, 2001. Photo courtesy of the FDNY Photo Unit.

Athletes

Mickey Mantle eulogy by Bob Costas courtesy of Bob Costas.

Arthur Ashe eulogy by Governor L. Douglas Wilder courtesy of Gov. Wilder.

Charles Atlas eulogy by Jerry Cowle courtesy of Jerry and Pauline Cowle. Originally appeared in *Sports Illustrated* magazine, June 11, 1979. Charles Atlas photo courtesy of Charles Atlas, Ltd.; © 2005 Charles Atlas, Ltd.; www.charlesatlas.com, P. O. Box D, Madison Square Station, New York, N.Y. 10159.

Wilt Chamberlain eulogy by Barbara Chamberlain Lewis courtesy of Barbara Chamberlain Lewis.

Christy Mathewson eulogy and photo courtesy of Eddie Frierson, Mathewson Foundation.

Parents

Col. Don Conroy eulogy by Pat Conroy courtesy of Pat Conroy.

Hilda Stegner eulogy by Wallace Stegner reprinted by permission of Brandt and Hochman, Literary Agents; © 1934 by Wallace Stegner.

Edith Freundlich eulogy by Peter Freundlich courtesy of Peter Freundlich. Edith Freundlich photo courtesy of Peter Freundlich and Andrew Freundlich.